Indian Diaspora Writer
SUNITI NAMJOSHI
A Voice of Radical Feminism

Indian Diaspora Writer
SUNITI NAMJOSHI
A Voice of Radical Feminism

SUMITA PURI

Prestige Books International
New Delhi

Published by
Prestige Books International
New Delhi 110 060
prestigebooks@gmail.com
Phones: 9818755529; 9810323134

Associate Office
11 B, Broomwood Road
London SW11 6HU, U.K.

Associate Office
P.O. Box 2250
Sydney 2001, Australia

ISBN: 978-81-943009-3-9

Printed in India

Contents

Preface

Literature of the Indian Diaspora introduced me to Suniti Namjoshi's literary oeuvre and Canadian feminist writing. Suniti Namjoshi's reworking of fairy tales and folklore made me venture further into the world of Canadian feminist writers revisiting traditional children's fantasy literature. I am truly indebted to my mentor and guide Professor Harish Narang for his unremitting assistance and guidance in pursuing my academic goals in life. I am deeply grateful to him for being a friend, philosopher and guide in the truest sense. Sincerest thanks to Dr. Suman Bala *masi* for all the love, support and sound advice in my academic voyage ever since she introduced me to the discipline.

My parents-in-law deserve a special mention for their incessant help and support in all ways possible! No expressions can suffice for thanking my father, Dr. Sat Pal, for instilling the Ulyssian spirit in me and my Mamaji, Dr. Chandra K. Jaggi, for teaching me to change adversity into opportunity. Heartfelt thanks to my mother Rajni Pal and brother Vikas Pal for their blessings and encouragement. The research would just not have been possible without the seamless efforts of my husband Tushar in inspiring me to aspire! Blessings and love to my daughter Harshita for all the emotional support that she lends and for truly respecting me as an individual. I owe endless thanks to Lakshay, my karmic son for helping me regain my self-confidence.

I have no words to thank my friend for the past two decades Dr. Jyoti Jakhar Dahiya, for standing by me through thick and thin. Her tremendous confidence in me has helped me sail through whenever I wavered. Thanks to my friends Dr. Brati Biswas, Ms. Madhuri Chawla and Dr. Madhumita Chakraborty for simply keeping their faith in me!

I cannot close these prefatory remarks without thanking Prestige Books International for bringing out this book so elegantly and expeditiously.

Introduction

Well, let's tell the truth
The cat charmed me.
The tree disarmed me and though the real people
Hadn't yet harmed me,
I thought that they would
given the chance. (Namjoshi 1991)

Introducing Suniti Namjoshi as a writer of the Indian Diaspora presently settled in England would only serve as a cursory sketch of the creator of a vast range of poetry, fables and fiction. In fact, the large number of her works marked by her alternate forms, open-mindedness and unorthodox standpoint make her a writer opposed to all forms of classification. Suniti Namjoshi's abandonment of authoritative positions and her declaration of her lesbian reality facilitate her personal and creative growth. Rejection of prestigious positions led her to investigate the nature of all forms of dominance—of class, race, gender and nationality and transgress them thereafter. This transgression becomes her key concern and with stylistic wit and inventiveness, Suniti Namjoshi offers the readers a non-conformist and deviant world through her works. Amalendu Bose avers that Suniti Namjoshi is one of the modern Indian poets along with Kamala Das and Nissim Ezekiel who "have the gift to produce striking poetry. . . . Poets like Roshen Alkazi, Kamala Das, Mary Erulkar, Nissim Ezekiel, Purshottam Lal, A.K. Ramanujan, Monika Varma; there are others who are on the authentic line: Noel Buckenham, Sukanta Chaudhuri, Ira De, Leela Dharmaraj, R. de L. Furtado, Lionel Gardner, Suniti Namjoshi, Saleem

Peeradina, Tilottama Rajan, P.K. Saha, Pradip Sen, Narendra K. Sethi, Shree Devi Singh, Kewlian Sio, Lalitha Venkateswaran, Sushila Yousufzaie. The best of these poets explore, without any perceptible evidence of strain, the infinite but cunningly elusive possibilities of the verbal medium—for the shades of new meanings and collocations that words are capable of acquiring are as ceaseless and dynamic as the unending chiaroscuro that plays on our paddy fields in late autumn." (Bose 56)

Born in Bombay, India, in 1941 Suniti Namjoshi joined the Indian Administrative Service in 1964 but soon left it. She went on to pursue a Master's degree in Public Administration at University of Missouri, Columbia. She completed her thesis on Ezra Pound at McGill University after migrating to Montreal in 1969. Having spent some time as a teacher at Scarborough College, University of Toronto, Suniti Namjoshi came under the influence of Christine Donald, her lesbian feminist friend who, in turn, helped her to fashion her feminist ideas and ideals. She left Toronto in 1987 to permanently settle down with her lesbian partner Gillian Hanscombe in Devon, England. In her own words:

> A major influence was my friend, Hilary Clare (alias Christine Donald). She had more brains than me, she could out-argue me and she had a literary mind. What's more I could see that she was fighting my battles for me, while I stood aside and did nothing; and that shamed me. She was active in both Women's Liberation and Gay Liberation. Up till then I thought that politics was something unpleasant that vaguely unpleasant people indulged in. I hadn't realized that it had something to do with ethics. I had also assumed that literature had nothing to do with power. It was books like Kate Millett's *Sexual Politics* and the work of writers like Virginia Woolf and Adrienne Rich that made me understand the extent to which sheer brutal power in the form of wealth and social ascendancy intersected with the literary enterprise and determined not just who could write what, but who could write at all and what constituted the literary canon. It wasn't just particular friends and im-

> portant writers that mattered though. There was the sense that a strong feminist movement existed, and for a writer this meant that there was an audience—a readership—to whom I might make sense. That was enormously exhilarating and it allowed me to think and explore and to write.

A poet, fabulist, myth-maker, fiction writer, feminist and a lesbian in the same breath, Suniti Namjoshi began her literary career with a book of poetry *Poems* published by the Writers Workshop, Calcutta in 1967. After this, she published numerous poems, fables, articles and reviews in India, Canada, United States and Britain. *Poems* was followed by *Cyclone in Pakistan* and *More Poems* (1971) which were also published in India. Vasant A. Shahane adds that the collection of poems is "marked by variety of theme and tone and the endeavour to endow commonplace realities and experiences with poetic significance." Namjoshi then wrote *Jackass and the Lady* in Canada between 1972 and 1976 which was published in India. Her first work published outside India was a collection of poems about death and childhood grief—*The Authentic Lie* (1982). *Feminist Fables* (1981) and *The Conversations of Cow* (1985) were published in London. By this time, Namjoshi had recognized her ideological and political stance as a lesbian feminist and had made it apparent in her works. The ensuing *Feminist Fables* was a prose work containing animals and figures from Western and Indian fables and folklore teaching human beings lessons in humanity. *The Conversations of Cow* concerned freewheeling identities of a lesbian cow named Bhadravati transforming into a woman, a white man and a Hindu goddess.

Retelling traditional tales to propose her feminist agenda becomes the prime motif of *Feminist Fables* that picks up several voices—of Cinderella, Rapunzel and the Red Riding Hood and of *From the Bedside Book of Nightmares* with voices of Caliban, Prospero, Miranda, Antigone and Penelope to comment on the victimization of women in heterosexual patriarchal hegemony. In 1986, Suniti Namjoshi published a collection of poems *Flesh and Paper* to articulate her lesbian reality. *The Blue Donkey Fables* followed in 1980 containing fables rife with animals—the blue donkey, the one-eyed monkey, the magpie and others—in order to satirize human frailties. *Because of India: Selected Poems and Fables* and *The Mothers of Maya Diip* were published in London in 1989. The former is divided into ten sections including poems and prose fables and the author's comments and views on them. The compositions witness a spatial-temporal sweep from India, Canada, United States of America and Great Britain over a period of twenty two years. *The Mothers of Maya Diip* finally introduces us to her posited vision of a feminist utopia—a dream of a matriarchal society where goodwill, peace and sisterhood will prevail. Apart from these, Suniti Namjoshi has produced *Aditi and the One-Eyed Monkey* (1986), *Building Babel* (1996) and *Goja: An Autobiographical Myth* (2000). In *Building Babel* Namjoshi picks up familiar vague "sisters" like Alice, Snow White, Red Riding Hood, Rose Green and others along with the creator-destroyer Crone-Kronos to fuse myth with cyber world in an attempt to build cultures. John Burnside writes: "*Building Babel* is most enjoyable—most interesting—when nothing is explained, when the archetypal creations do not stride to the front of the stage and address their audience. Of course, the stories are only the vehicles by which Namjoshi intends to convey her ideas—ideas which are complex and thought-provoking; nevertheless, the danger in beginning a story, only to confound it with philosophical or ideological speculation, is that the interest of the reader lies in the telling of the tale, and not in the ideas. The truth is, a good story is worth any amount of abstract thought, because stories transcend ideas (Burnside 382). *Sycorax: New Fables and Poems*, *The Fabulous Feminist: A Suniti Namjoshi Reader*, *Suki* and *Foxy Aesop aka*

Aesop the Fox are her latest contribution to the literary scene. Her contributions to children's literature further include *Aditi and the Thames Dragon, Aditi and the Marine Sage, Aditi and the Techno Sage, Aditi and Her Friends Take on the Vesuvian Giant, Aditi and Her Friends Meet Grendel, Gardy in the City of Lions, Monkeyji and the Word Eater, Blue and Other Stories, Little I* and many others. Apart from these she has also translated *Poems of Govindagraj* by Ram Ganesh Gadkari in collaboration with Sarojini Namjoshi.

Suniti Namjoshi's employment of fantasy, myth-making and fabulation have enabled her to postulate the lesbian feminist perspective developed over the years of her stay in the United States, Canada and Great Britain. The impact of her contemporary Canadian feminists engaged in their efforts of changing the status quo by reworking conventional stories was deep enough to instigate her to make her contribution to the same. So, she picked her heroines from the Indian and Western literature and moulded them as strong characters rebelling against patriarchal subjugation. The book analyzes Suniti Namjoshi's works to assess her use of myths and fusion of genres from Indian and Western folklore by way of following her Canadian feminist contemporaries to direct the attention of the readers towards her views on women's suppression in a male-governed society. Further, her dislocation as an Indian diasporic writer in the United States, Canada and lastly to Britain serves as a basis of her writing despite her blatant refusal to portray the immigrant experience in her works. The postcolonial diasporic writer, in due course of her literary journey, affirms that India and her Indianness have not only shaped her identity but also helped her deviate from the normative: "I don't think of diaspora as home. . . . India is not something anyone can give or take away from me . . . what ties one to India, even when one does not want to be tied are a thousand strands." Her transnational position is further validated by the statement: "now my attitude is that all these places are mine for they have given me something and I have tried to give them something in return." (Vevaina 200-1)

The book is divided into four comprehensive chapters to explicate feminism and lesbian feminist theory exclusively. The first chapter is dedicated to the history and politics of feminism as a progressive movement and a belief system. The chapter opens with a discourse on 'Feminism' as a state of protest against women on social, economic and ideological grounds. Feminism as a movement began with the struggle for the right to vote and expanded its horizon to incorporate issues regarding reproductive rights, child care, equal wages for equal work and equal human rights in all spheres of life. Numerous organizations were set up to expose the artifice of patriarchal system that positions men as superior to women. The delineation is followed by tracing the roots of feminism from the first voice raised for the cause of women by Mary Wollstonecraft in *A Vindication of the Rights of Women* in 1792 to the fruition of feminisms—Liberal Feminism, Cultural Feminism, Socialist Feminism and so on. The focus is then oriented towards the study of the struggles of various theorists such as Simone de Beauvoir, Kate Millett and Elaine Showalter to comprehend the polemics of sexual politics that, in turn, forms the basis of caste, race and nationality. The biological difference is at the core of the cultural construction of the 'masculine' and 'feminine' gender codes. As a result, women have been ascribed with the notions of passivity, humility and submissiveness. The harassment of women is because they are women, the men's 'Other.'

Feminist criticism threw light on the fact that women are denied a definite status in the literary arena and are even forbidden from proving their creative potential. The reading of Mary Ellman, Sandra Gilbert and Susan Gubar enable us to discern that women have been projected as the clichéd angel or the monster and have had to conform to the patriarchal model in their writing as well. The chapter further looks at the feminist struggle in Canada after getting the first insights into feminist theory. Canadian feminist theorists, writers and activists have taken tremendous pains in their goal of CR or consciousness-raising and reformation of women in society. The history of women's movement in Canada is then divided into its 'first' and 'second' wave. The experiences of Margaret Atwood, Anne Cameron, Barbara Godard and others unearthed women's victimization on the basis of sexual, economic and socio-cultural difference.

The central section traces the 'first wave' with the growth of 'Institutionalized Feminism' and 'Grass-roots Feminism.' The rise of feminist groups that concretized in the 'second wave' as Socialist, Liberal, Cultural and Radical Feminisms is outlined thereafter. Beginning with equal rights and suffrage, feminists organized as Liberal feminists to point out that laws made by men are predominantly in favour of their own sex and restrict the freedom of women. The liberal feminists strived for changes in legal rights for women including the right to abortion and day-care facilities. The socialist feminists felt that the fundamental structural social patterns need to be changed as it is the social constructs of gender, class and race that act as a hindrance in the way of women's emancipation. Feminists revolted against poverty, unequal pay and even unpaid work. This group firmly upheld capitalism as the root cause of oppression making women reliant on their male counterparts. Man, as the earning partner, arrogates himself the power to hegemonize and reduce woman to a servile position. Radical feminists further expounded that the servility of women in patriarchy can be done away with if women shun patriarchy completely to organize a universal female culture. Marriage and love encourage subordination and should be entirely forsaken.

Radical feminism gave birth to Cultural Feminism that sought a more humane view of the world free from sexual abuse. The politics of discrimination is centred on the culturally laid gender codes rather than the biological sex. The Lesbian Feminist movement in Canada perceived women as independent of the heteronormative societal structures. An important section is dedicated to the evolution and growth of lesbian groups such as LOOT and National Lesbian Forum. Lesbian feminist theory also led to the clarification that lesbians are not only two women engaged in a sexual relationship but also women who share quality time, feelings and experiences outside the shackles of patriarchy. The lesbian feminists, therefore, theorized that separatism is the final answer to all the problems of women.

The second chapter elucidates the embedment of gender constructs in traditional tales. Theories proposed by Bruno Bettelheim, Gretchen Sankey and others contest the popular notion that fairy and folk tales are innocent narratives passed on to children. The perception is thus challenged to expose the adverse impact on children. It is then pointed out how feminist writers in Canada strive to break the stereotypical projections of women in children's fiction. With the inputs from theorists discussed in the previous chapter, the emphasis shifts to the study of the breaking of classical archetypes of women as 'pretty,' 'humble,' 'chaste,' 'meek' and so on. This 'sexist criticism' is alternately contested in the refashioning of myths, fables and fairy tales by Canadian feminist writers such as Virginia Lee Hines, Elizabeth Greene and Pauline Rankin. These writers pick traditional tales of Cinderella, The Little Mermaid, Rapunzel along with the classical myth of Eve to present women as 'pickled' and 'preserved' for the male gaze in literature. They flip the accepted narratives to depict women as potential human beings with courage and resolution. The fabulist voices of Canada display their creativity by designing strong images of women as defying the said norms and subsequently seeking solace in lesbian intimacy.

The next chapter focusses on the Indian and Western influence as reflected in Suniti Namjoshi's literary oeuvre. The selection of Indian narratives further corroborates that Suniti's Indian roots permeate her writing regardless of her negation of the rendering of the Indian diasporic dilemma in her creations. Namjoshi's lesbian feminist perspective places her in the Western as opposed to the Indian writing tradition and yet her recourse to Indian philosophy makes that impossible as well. Hence, Namjoshi's works make her recognized as a writer beyond categorizable limits. A lesbian from India influenced by Western feminist theory, Suniti Namjoshi shows evidence of both her Indian and lesbian reality in her works. In an interview with Kausalya Santhanam published in *The Hindu*, Suniti admits: "one does not know why a writer's mind works in a certain way. It just does. The reason may be that I have grown up in India. Here, every time someone asks a question, the answer is in the form of a story. We are a nation of storytellers. If one wants to answer questions, the fable is a good form, for it is didactic and helps in dealing with issues such as racism, gender stereotyping and attitudes towards exploitation of the planet."

The impact of Hindu philosophy can be seen in bringing up of the Hindu concept of fluidity of identity as well as the transgression of sexual boundaries. Namjoshi combines her understanding of Hinduism with the Western separatist ideology to paint a unique world inhabited by women in a position of power and men in a position of inferiority. In league with her Canadian colleagues, Suniti Namjoshi picks up conventional heroines and then inverts their portrayals to authenticate her lesbian feminist identity. She presents women in the three stages designated by Elaine Showalter as the 'Feminine,' 'Feminist' and the 'Female.' Through the rewriting of fables and fairy tales, Namjoshi theorizes how heterosexuality ascribes negative/ passive roles to women forcing them to hold their tongues. The transgression of gender constructs can liberate themselves from suppression in order to discover their real strength. Her radical views are fully articulated in her utopian model of a fictional matriarchal world reducing men to be extremely insignificant and incapable beings.

The last chapter is an extensive discourse on the two significant texts *Feminist Fables* and *The Mothers of Maya Diip* by Suniti Namjoshi to critically review her depiction of women's oppression and the proposed solution of a lesbian feminist utopia. Her works reflect a hope for a better society based on improved man-woman relationships, resistance to heteronormativity, legitimacy for nonconformist sexual relations, realization of women's potential and separatism for women. The desire to authenticate her radical tenets makes her a writer refusing to conform to traditional modes of writing and the invention of new strategies of narration and style. Suniti Namjoshi's exportation of Western and Indian ideologies mingled with her wit, jocularity and sarcasm posit a humane world marked with a celebration of womanhood. The book conclusively validates the separatist ideology operative in Canadian writing and in the literary works of Suniti Namjoshi.

History and Politics of Canadian Feminism/ Feminisms

The historical politics or the political history of women's emancipation has to customarily begin with the complex task of comprehending the nuanced term feminism or feminisms—the definitions and interpretations proposed so far, ranging from the state of exercising one's will to establishing one's identity and further the fight against the power relations between men and women. The movement has been global as women formed groups across nations raised their voice against the hegemonic heteronormative society. The protest addressed as Feminism has been used as an umbrella term to describe those men and women who felt the need to fight against the oppression of women on social, economic, and ideological grounds, according to Jeremy Hawthorn in *A Glossary of Contemporary Literary Theory*. The panoramic agitation is further classified as 'Feminine,' 'Feminist' and 'Female' by Elaine Showalter in *A Literature of Their Own: British Women Novelists from Bronte to Lessing*. She elucidates that first, there is a prolonged phase of *imitation* of the prevailing modes of the dominant tradition, and *internalization* of its standards of art and its views on social roles. Second, there is a phase of *protest* against these values, and *advocacy* of minority rights and values, including a demand for autonomy. Finally, there is a phase of *self-discovery*, a turning inward freed from the dependency of opposition, a search for identity. An appropriate terminology for women writers is to call these stages, *Feminine, Feminist,* and *Female*. (Qtd Moi 1985: 56) For Toril Moi, 'Femaleness' is a biological fact, 'Femininity,' a set of culturally defined attributes, and 'Feminism' a political position. (1989: 117-32)

The inequity in patriarchy is simply due to the fact that women are women, the men's 'Other,' in Simone de Beauvoir's words. In the nascent stages, the feminists strived for a utopian state where both the sexes are treated equally, where women are in a position to assert and affirm their selves rather than being defined by and as the 'Other.' The next phase of theorists deliberated on the issue whether this 'Promised Land' was the actual aim of feminism. Feminist writers disputed that no such state is viable and that equality should be accompanied with the realization that men and women are different and that neither is subservient to the other.

In relation to the above, feminist critics exposed, that women have not only been denied a status in society, but have also been deprived of it in literature and history as well. Feminist criticism posited a feminist reading to look at the various images of women depicted in literature, whether it is the angel or the monster, Sati-Savitri or Kali. It projects the psyche of the women as readers and writers, and looks at their history, themes, and styles exclusively termed as 'Gynocritics' by Elaine Showalter. Mary Ellman revealed the sexist criticism or "phallic criticism" in literature—how literature by women has been considered as an examination of their body parts by male critics and writers. She says: "books by women are treated as though they themselves were women, and criticism embarks, at its happiest upon an intellectual measuring of busts and hips." (*Ibid.* 33) As a discipline, Feminist Criticism does not exist in isolation. It draws upon various schools of thought such as Marxism, Psycho-analysis, Structuralism, Existentialism, Deconstruction and so on which can be seen in the readings of the major feminist theorists such as Simone de Beauvoir, Luce Irigaray, Julia Kristeva, Kate Millett and many more.

The first voice in modern times in favour of women's rights was in 1792 with the publication of Mary Wollstonecraft's *A Vindication of the Rights of Woman*, where she argues for women's education and protection by law. She demands that women should first be treated as human beings. She writes:

> Dismissing then, those petty feminine phrases, which the men condescendingly use to soften our slavish dependence, and despising that weak elegance of mind, exquisite sensibility, and sweet docility of manners, supposed to be the sexual characteristics of the weaker vessel. I wish to show that elegance is inferior to virtue, that the first object of laudable ambition is to obtain a character as a human being, regardless of the distinction of sex, and that secondary views should be brought to this simple touchstone. (Arora 18)

During the seventeenth and eighteenth centuries, it was assumed that the place of women was at home as wives and mothers. With the industrial revolution, women became all the more confined to homes as only men went outside to earn. The male liberal theorists of the eighteenth century advocated that women should restrict themselves to familial cares only. Mary Wollstonecraft and other theorists argued that women were citizens, human beings, who should enjoy the same basic rights as men. Wollstonecraft contended that women should cultivate their powers of critical thinking that will, in turn, enable them to develop their souls. Liberal feminists following her urged that laws made by men are deliberate attempts to crush women's individuality. In 1869, John Stuart Mill raised the issue of women's rights in *The Subjection of Women*. He fought for their education and individual liberty and freedom. Mill used the utilitarian philosophy of the 'greatest good for the greatest number' to justify that if women are liberated, half the human race is liberated, and so, happiness to women will bring the highest happiness to mankind.

As a movement, Feminism began in the United States in the 1960s with the granting of franchise to women. The publication of Betty Friedan's *The Feminine Mystique* took the American society by storm. She defined feminism thus: "My definition of feminism is simply that women are people in the fullest sense of the word, who must be free to move in society with all the privileges and opportunities and responsibilities that are their human right." (Qtd. Burt 37)

Women participated in the Civil Rights Movement and formed their own liberal groups to extend their protest against subservience to men. In 1970, women's organizations such as NOW (National Organization for Women) were set up for fighting their own battle for self-fulfillment in a male-governed society. The pioneering works: Virginia Woolf's *A Room of One's Own*, Mary Ellman's *Thinking about Women*, Elaine Showalter's *A Literature of Their Own: British Women Novelists from Bronte to Lessing* and Kale Millett's *Sexual Politics* sowed the first seeds of feminist writing and criticism. The major aim of the feminist critic was to fight for social and political change, for a better status and equal rights for women in society.

In 1929, Virginia Woolf published *A Room of One's Own* hoping for a separate space for women, where they can enhance their creative potential. She pointed out that feminism is a fight against male tyranny in the patriarchal set-up that disparages women. Women have been looked down upon by men in order to prove their heroic stature. They have served as looking glasses in which men see themselves twice their natural size. Women need to enhance their creative and critical powers if they want to change the value system. Subsequently, Mary Ellman exposed the sexist or 'phallic criticism' in literature. Kate Millett's *Sexual Politics* defined sexual politics as "the process whereby the ruling sex seeks to maintain and extend its power over the subordinate sex." (Qtd. Moi 1985: 26) Patriarchy, thus, has been a mode of this sexual politics and domination and has denied basic human rights to women, making them subservient to men.

In the early 1970s a collection of essays by various feminists entitled *Images of Women in Fiction: Feminist Perspectives* exposed female stereotypes in male writing. Elaine Showalter argued that the focus of feminist criticism should be exclusively on women's writing. In the late 1970s three major works appeared on the literary scene that caused a lot of furore: Elaine Showalter's *A Literature of Their Own: British Women Novelists from Bronte to Lessing*, Ellen Moers' *The Literary Women* and Sandra Gilbert and Susan Gubar's *The Madwoman in the Attic*. Moers' book reflected that women's writing is not a sub-group in the history of literature. According to her, women have been largely excluded from the canon and in order to understand the history of literature, one must know the history of women's writing as well. Elaine Showalter, on the other hand, contended that women have never had a concrete movement in literature as they have made renewed attempts in finding a position in society in every generation. She recorded the three stages, the 'Feminine,' 'Feminist' and 'Female' in the historical development of women's writing. For her, the feminine period began with the appearance of women writers using male pseudonyms in 1840s till the death of George Eliot in 1880. The feminist phase was from 1880 to 1920, a state of protest for rights, and the female stage from 1920 onwards, with a new turn in the 1960s, a phase of self-discovery. Sandra Gilbert and Susan Gubar indicated that women have not enjoyed the freedom to create their own images in literature since they have had to conform to patriarchal norms. Women's images as the angel or the monster, the sweet heroine and the mad woman are products of male fantasy as creativity is considered predominantly a male's domain. The two theorists wished that their works will enable them to retrieve the lost female unity and create a better world for women.

Whereas Elaine Showalter, Mary Ellman, Sandra Gilbert, Susan Gubar, Kate Millett and others contributed to the women's movement in the United States, the theories proposed by Simone de Beauvoir, Julia Kristeva, Luce Irigaray and others brought revolution in France. In 1949, Simone de Beauvoir published *The Second Sex* and revealed that women have been objectified by men, constructed as the 'Other' in patriarchy and denied subjectivity. Patriarchal ideology has reduced them to 'inauthentic' objects, which needs to be changed. She also declared that, one is not born, but rather becomes a woman. Femininity is a social construct and a woman is not born passive or submissive but becomes so under the pressures of society and culture. She writes: "In my definition, feminists are women or even men, too—who are fighting to change women's condition, in association with the class struggle, but independent of it as well, without making the changes they strive for totally dependent on changing the society as a whole." (*Ibid.* 91-92)

French Feminism was actually born with the student revolt of May 1968 in Paris. Following their American sisters, women in France formed women-only groups such as 'Psychanalyse et Politique.' Freudian psychoanalysis became the basis of their struggle in exploring the unconscious of women with publication of Juliet Mitchell's *Psychoanalysis and Feminism* in 1974. Between 1975 and 1977, Hélène Cixous published a lot of theoretical works translated into English as *The Laugh of the Medusa*, *Castration or Decapitation* and so on. For Cixous, feminists are women who strive for social legitimization. She analyzed that, in mainly all binary oppositions, activity/ passivity, father/ mother, head/ emotions, intelligible/ sensitive, the underlying opposition is man/ woman and woman has been perceived as secondary, passive and powerless. In her utopian vision, women will get rid of this logocentric ideology that silences women and will become creative in a non-oppressive and non-sexist society. She also opposed the term *Écriture féminine* or 'feminine writing' as terms like 'feminine' and 'masculine' are rooted in sexual difference. For her, the work holds more significance than the sex of the author.

In the 1970s, another feminist theorist shot to fame in France by linking psychoanalysis and feminism. Luce Irigaray, a psychoanalyst by profession, produced a number of theoretical writings including *The Language of Dementia*, *This Sex which is not One* and *Speculum of the Other Woman.* Following Freudian psychoanalysis, she said that women lack the male organ, the phallus which is the symbol of power. So she is posited as the man's 'other,' an 'other' who is absent, negative, or at best, lesser than man. Her subjectivity is repressed in patriarchal discourse and like Woolf's looking glass, she becomes a mirror for his own masculinity. Irigaray upheld that women are not equal but different. So they must fight, not for equality, but for a separate space in society. She spoke of a specific women's language, which she called *'parler femme'* or 'womanspeak.' If women want to change the existing order, they ought to unite and form women-only groups to voice their inner feelings and desires outside patriarchy. While Irigaray sought a language for women, Kristeva exposes the sexism in language. In *Man Made Language*, Dale Spender asserts: "The English language has been literally man made and . . . it is still primarily under male control. . . . This monopoly over language is one of the means by which males have ensured their own primacy, and consequently have ensured the invisibility or 'other' nature of females, and this primacy is perpetuated while women continue to use, unchanged the language which we have inherited." (Qtd. Moi 1985: 156)

For Irigaray, femininity is that which is marginalized by the patriarchal symbolic order. So women are perceived as 'feminine' or subverted and marginalized by the social order and even language becomes a tool of this subversion.

Women's fight for liberation has led to the emergence of various branches or schools of thought. The end of the twentieth century witnessed the rise of Radical Feminism with Kate Millett, Shulamith Firestone, Ann Oakley, Eva Figes, Barbara Burris and many more. Radical feminists believed that sex is the prime basis of discrimination. Shulamith Firestone, Anne Koedt, Diane Crothers and Cellestine Ware issued a manifesto entitled "Politics of the Ego" in 1970 articulating the view: "that women's oppression is rooted primarily in psychological, not economic, factors." (Qtd. Donavan 143) Barbara Burris and other radical feminists, in their essay, "The Fourth World Manifesto" contended that women all over the world form a caste which is "colonized" by male "imperialism." Women have been suppressed and their liberation is only possible if they organize as women. Burris added: "we identify with all women all races, classes and countries all over the world. The female culture is the Fourth World." (*Ibid.* 144)

It was Kate Millett's *Sexual Politics* and Shulamith Firestone's *The Dialectic of Sex: The Case of Feminist Revolution* that fully articulated the radical feminist theory. Millett pointed out that family is the origin of patriarchal subjugation. Family lays down prescribed roles and status of women when they are young which are embedded forever. Man has power biologically, so he rules over woman. So 'sex' becomes the basis of 'gender' difference. Institutions such as marriage and love should be discarded as they promote dependence on men. Radical feminism is, therefore, a journey or process of "women becoming." It is a voyage from this world to another where women will be able to free themselves from the demons of patriarchy. This power of "women becoming" is termed as 'gynergy' by Mary Daly. So, the radical feminists ask women not to submit to men. They have their own lives to live and should even consider childbirth as voluntary.

Radical feminism gave birth to various forms of feminisms, the earliest being Cultural Feminism. As early as at the end of the nineteenth century a group of women went beyond women's rights to a broader cultural transformation. These women were labelled as cultural feminists who fought for the preservation of female virtues, similar to Virginia Woolf's Outsider's Society in *Three Guineas.* Cultural feminism initiated with Margaret Fuller's *Women in the Nineteenth Century*. Fuller believed that women must seek self-reliance and freedom from all kinds of bondage in patriarchy. She promoted the idea of female bonding and self-discovery:

> Women must leave off asking [men] and being influenced by them, but retire within themselves, and explore the groundwork of life till they find their peculiar secret. Then, when they come forth again, renovated and baptized, they will know how to turn all dross to gold. (*Ibid*. 34)

Cultural feminists argue that women are not only denied opportunities in their work place but also that their ideas are perceived as 'stupid' and 'childish.' Another cultural feminist, Stanton pointed out that the feminine and masculine elements were united in one person previously and to re-unite them, one needs to pray to a "Heavenly Mother" in addition to the "Heavenly Father." These feminists do not consider the source of this difference between men and women as biological, but cultural. To seek a humane worldview, these destructive masculine ideologies must be negated. Just as women preserve these feminine virtues or women's culture at home, they can revolutionize the public sphere with these values as well.

In the 1980s, the coloured women formed their own group called the Black feminists who condemned the radical feminists to be racists. Black feminists railed against the women's movement that had been primarily for the white women. They argued that their experiences were different from those of the white women which could not be ignored. They formed their own groups such as the Combahee River Collective and were concerned with the establishment of a feminism which would include race, ethnicity and class differences along with sex as the basis of their analysis of women's oppression.

Black feminists revealed how black women have been victims of exploitation and objectification more than their white sisters. Noted Black feminist Beale showed how they have been physically raped and compelled to serve as the white woman's maids when their own children were starving. Bell Hooks exposed the myth of matriarchy in black women. The black woman has served the 'Other' in a white patriarchal society who can be gazed at, and dominated because of her sex and race. Bell Hooks' *Ain't I a Woman: Black Women and Feminism?*, Cherríe Moraga and Gloria Anzaldúa's edited *This Bridge Called My Back: Writings by Radical Women of Color* contributed to the black feminist movement. Another important aspect of black feminism was the concern for retaining their racial and ethnic roots. Alice Walker's *In Search of Our Mothers' Gardens*: *Womanist Prose* was the first step in preserving the culture and history of their mothers. The Black feminists had to choose between a white patriarchal world and a brown matriarchal world and the choice in favour of the latter was at the heart of their struggle.

Like the women of colour, lesbians felt that they are double victims of oppression—being women as well as homosexuals. The word 'homosexual' was first used in the year 1870 and 'same-sex sex' or 'gays' and 'lesbians' were, however, adapted by people to address these people. Till the late nineteenth century, homosexuality was banned as criminal law and considered a subject for medicine and psychiatry. So, SF also rendered the homosexual stereotype as an effeminate caricature, a 'soul-sick lesbian,' a man-eating Amazon or a blood-thirsty vampire, as pointed out by Pearson (3). It was only in 1967 that homosexuality was decriminalized in England, and in the United States the law varies from state to state. It has been decriminalized eventually in India on 6 September 2018. In 1973, the American Psychiatry Association declared it to be a mental disorder and attempts to cure it, through hormonal treatment or castration, went on for long. Contemporary Lesbian feminism first emerged with the theories laid down by the "Radicalesbians," a New York group in their article "The Woman Identified Woman," defining 'lesbian' as "the woman, who, often, beginning at an extremely early age, acts in accordance with her inner compulsion to be a more complete and freer human being than her society cares to allow her." (Donavan 161)

In 1969 and 1970, Martha Shelley urged that the lesbian should be used as a model of the independent woman. Women need to develop their identity with reference to themselves and not to men. They have to be "womanidentified," loved and supported in a world devoid of men. Each lesbian is a feminist, for she protests against all forms of male bondage and takes responsibility for her own actions. Lesbian feminists also focused on retrieving their own history; showing relationships between women prevalent in literature. Carol Smith-Rosenberg and Lillian Faderman have traced such friendships between nineteenth century American women and Renaissance women respectively. The Leeds Revolutionary Feminist Group, in "The Case against Heterosexuality" proposed the utopian model for lesbians based in separatism as a final solution to the problems of women in a male-dominated society. They contended that women have to overthrow the male system and withdraw from it for good.

Whereas the cultural feminist adapted a totally pacifist approach in the conversion of society, and the radical feminist fumed with anger, the liberal feminists strived for equal participation of women in all walks of life including war. This group of activists toiled for the freedom of enjoyment of women's rights and opportunities. They upheld that it is the biological determinism of women as socially inferior, that they are suited to certain kinds of work and not fit for others, which form the reasons for this discrimination. Women are given low wages in service and considered solely responsible for childcare and household work, due to which they are denied opportunities in other spheres of life. They are viewed as sex objects and are restrained in their dress and behaviour. They are prohibited from wandering in public spaces for fear of sexual assault. Patriarchy limits their intellectual faculties as they are said to be safer at home and denied permission to get exposed to public life. Feminists of this group aim at freeing women from this tyrannical dependent status in patriarchy. Thus, members of Liberal feminism group fight for inclusion of women as decision makers—at home, in the workplace and in all other matters. Justice, equal rights, equal wages, and right to child-birth, liberation from all kinds of sexual and economic dependence are their goals.

Apart from the aforementioned, another group that emerged called themselves the Socialist feminists who upheld that capitalism is the root cause of oppression. Man, in a capitalist society, becomes the bourgeoisie and woman becomes the proletariat. Since man is the bread earner, he earns and the work of a woman at home does not give her money, and gives her an inferior position. Socialist feminists following Simone de Beauvoir wished for a social change where women will enjoy a defined and definite status in the public sphere. Women will contribute as wage earners to the household and demand division of labour at home. Women's work at home has never been considered valuable and worthy of wages. So the first task is to abolish capitalism according to this group including Eli Zaretsky, Ann Foreman, Zillah R. Eisenstein and so on.

Women must also demand their rights and privileges as mothers and carriers of cultural values. Feminists of this group, thus, fought for a women's culture rooted in women's experience and practice that will enable them to build a society free from all forms of patriarchal and class-based oppression. In the words of Ann Ferguson and Nancy Folbre; it is "the establishment of a self-defined revolutionary *feminist women's culture* which can be ideologically and materially support women 'outside patriarchy.' Counter-hegemonic cultural and material support networks can provide woman-identified substitutes for patriarchal production." (*Ibid.* 86)

As the women's liberation movement challenged stereotypes, protested against rape, sexual abuse, and domestic violence and provided varied reasons responsible for the gender inequity in society, they have also had to contest the ideology of the Biological Essentialists who argue that the differences in men and women are primarily because of genetic make-up. Therefore, we are, simply what we are because of our biological differences and our behaviour and preferences are also biologically pre-defined. So women are naturally and essentially loving, caring, giving, emotional and passive whereas men are essentially violent, aggressive, rational and dominant. Gender Studies by theorists like Ann Oakley and Judith Butler refute this hypothetical stance by elucidating the performative aspect of gender roles in society. Ann Oakley was the first one to differentiate sex from gender. In *Sex, Gender and Society* Oakley defines sex as anatomical and gender as a product, not of biology, but of the social, cultural and psychological codes around girls and boys. These codes are palpable in the perceptions, dress codes, toys and even books for children. Butler, on the other hand, considers both sex and gender as cultural constructs. She avers that barring the anatomy, the human body does not have a pre-defined sex. When a baby is born, the society designates the sex as a boy or a girl that consequently initiates the process of becoming a boy or a girl and the performance as masculine or feminine.

Feminism today becomes interdisciplinary and feminist critics incorporate other theories such as Marxism, Postcolonialism, Gender Theory etc. to do textual analysis. For instance, a postcolonial feminist would look at the portrayal of white vs. non-white female characters in literary texts and a Marxist would see class as the basis of discrimination along with gender. It also looks at construction of gender across genres—short story, novel, poetry, media, magazines, television soap operas, block buster movies—romance, thrillers, advertisements, science fiction and so on. The focus of postmodern theorists is the deconstruction of the stereotype of image of woman and the reconstruction of woman's identity, ever-changing in the modern times. The major theorists and critics are Susan Faludi—*Backlash: The Undeclared War against American Women*, Judith Butler—*Gender Trouble*, Angela McRobbie—*Feminism and Youth Culture: From 'Jackie' to 'Just Seventeen*,' Toril Moi—*Sexual/ Textual Politics: Feminist Literary Theory*, Naomi Wolf—*The Beauty Myth* and so on. To conclude, feminism or feminisms have been politicized throughout history to locate women's problems on numerous grounds. Yet, the collective fight is on to project men and women not as equal but, in fact, as different and neither as submissive to the other. Since patriarchy relegates women to an inferior position socially, economically, and culturally, women and men must strive to realize that the sexual difference must not be the basis of social difference and hence gender constructs should be done away with completely.

"One is not born, but becomes a woman," said Simone de Beauvoir in *The Second Sex*. The becoming of a woman, the process whereby a female discovers her 'self,' her womanhood, her search for identity and its assertion, has been reasoned out by feminists time and again. Before women fought for their rights, women were tutored to behave properly, to be good wives, and to act like 'women' with the attributes of humility, docility, meekness to the extent of being stupid and weak. They were not allowed to debate on issues like Abortion, Lesbianism, incest and so on. With the advent of the feminist movements in the 1960s and 1970s, the scenario changed. Women were encouraged to be active and aware of their rights and duties. They began to comprehend how they have been suppressed, oppressed and repressed by hegemonic forces in society. They brought to the fore that writing by women has been condemned as weak, subjective, confessional and narcissistic. Masculine and feminine roles started being questioned and debated openly. They began exposing social taboos and started writing boldly about their experiences. Margaret Atwood remarks in an article titled "If You Can't Say Something Nice, Don't Say Anything at All":

> Women of my generation were told not to hobble with our high heels and our panty girdles on. We were told endlessly: *thou shalt not*. We don't need to hear it again, and especially not for women. Feminism has done many good things for many women writers, but surely the most important has been the permission to say the unsaid, to encourage women to claim their full humanity, which means acknowledging the shadows as well as the lights.

Feminism in Canada marked a struggle for such strong voices that can enable women to contest their fears and apprehensions and to protest against their silencing. It became a movement enabling them to express their feelings openly. The feminists state that patriarchy has played a very crucial role in making women afraid of men and denying them their identity and status. Women grow up emotionally, financially and sexually dependent on men. Feminism advocates the overthrow of such fears and helps them to make forward steps in the path of emancipation. Since time immemorial, men have dictated what women should do, think, feel, want and need. Women must try to make amends, as Anne Cameron, a noted Canadian writer, puts it:

> I know . . . that patriarchy condones and encourages the physical, emotional, psychological and sexual abuse of children to ensure that we all grow up frightened and afraid to trust others. I am convinced we cannot 'repair' or 'fix' the present system, and must openly advocate the overthrow of the bullshit. To me, that is feminism. (66)

What does, then, a feminist text do to a reader? How does a feminist reader react to such a text? Such questions also formed a crucial aspect of feminist criticism in Canada. When a reader reads a feminist piece of writing, she tries to grasp the writer's life, the experiences of the protagonist, and tries to identify her biological identity with other women. She attempts at unravelling the hidden meaning in the text and learns to look at it with a new critical direction. "Acknowledging this rich silence informing the female text is to validate our experience as women," says Barbara Godard. Feminist criticism points out that women's fiction raises theoretical issues and challenges the traditional notions about women and their creative potential. Once again, in Barbara Godard's words: "Women's (re)writing interrupts conventional meanings of 'fiction' and 'theory' which assign different truth values to discourses. Established meanings become suspect: the theory as fiction, fictionalysis, advances narrative truths, partial, provisional, making no claims to universality. This incites the reader to rethink her/ his presence within 'social reality' and disturbs those constructions that work at keeping us all in our 'proper' places." (119)

The contemporary women's movement in Canada originated on two different lines. On the one hand, there were women who were professionals from trained and traditional institutions who sought better opportunities for women. On the other hand, there were women from homes and universities who were mainly into raising the consciousness of other women and organizing social groups to educate them about their rights. The former current, previously known as Institutionalized Feminism, gradually transformed into Liberal Feminism, while the latter is often referred to as Grass-roots Feminism.

The First-wave of feminism is marked as the period from 1840s to 1920s dealing primarily with the issues of Suffrage, Birth Control, Education, Equal rights and Legal Protection. In the Second-wave, from the 1960s to 1980s, the women's organizations were concerned with the issues of granting of the franchise to women, reproductive rights, women's health, better work conditions, social recognition and protest against domestic violence, rape, sexual assault, and child sexual abuse. From the 1980s onwards, corresponding with the Third-wave of feminism, the struggle had been the inclusion of class, race, ethnicity, and nationality.

The First-wave of feminism in Canada was seen in the earliest women's movement in which women organized together to fight for issues such as suffrage, education, pregnancy and abortion rights, economic independence and so on. The first step towards a progressive woman's movement was seen in the first Canadian suffrage organization founded by Dr. Emily Howard Stowe in Toronto in 1876. Social reformers all over Canada joined hands and successfully obtained the provincial franchise by 1922.

The granting of the suffrage marks the culmination of the First-wave of feminism in Canada. Yet, it was not only the right to vote that mattered to the feminists of this phase. Women remained active between 1920 and 1960 which was a transition phase from women's movement to the modern feminist movement. One of the major concerns of the feminists of this time was to understand the changing role of women as 'mothers'—a movement that is now referred to as Maternal Feminism. In the words of the maternal feminism's foremost advocate, Nellie McClung: "The woman movement . . . is a spiritual revival of the best instincts of womanhood—the instinct to serve and save the race. . . . Women are naturally the guardians of the race, and every normal woman desires children. . . . It is women's place to lift high the standard of morality." (Qtd. Adamson 31)

Apart from suffrage and equal rights, women need to and should consider it a moral obligation to rear children in the best manner possible in order to reform the society. In an endeavour to bring in this reform, women need better facilities, reproductive rights and nurturing. The maternal feminists argued that women's role, thus, becomes morally superior to men, as they are not only the guardians of the family but also of the public morality at large. This great task of 'mothering,' as a strong commitment on the part of women in Canada, was put forward by Lady Aberdeen of the National Council of Women in Canada. This sense of moral superiority of women in society sowed the seeds of radical feminism in the Second-wave of feminism in Canada.

The second major argument of the First-wave feminists was that women should enjoy equal rights as men. The focus of this group of feminists as the equal-rights feminists was the cognition of human rights as universal irrespective of gender. The first expression of this struggle was seen in the efforts of the Dr. Emily Howard Stowe's Toronto Women's Literary Club in 1876 which took the name of Toronto Women's Suffrage Association in 1883. Although the prime concern of this equal-rights feminists group was the granting of suffrage, it also fought for providing improved educational opportunities to women. Stowe argued that woman should be "as free to choose her vocation as her brother, tethered by no conventionalities, enslaved by no chains either of her own or man's forging." (*Ibid.* 33)

Another noted equal-rights feminist Flora Macdonald Denison of the First-wave of feminism took active part in the Toronto suffrage movement and fought for birth control and divorce rights. She led the Canadian Suffrage Association from 1911 to 1914 and worked with many social reformers in the struggle for equal human rights. She argued that: "men and women should be born equally free and independent members of the human race." (Ibid. 33) Equal-rights feminism and the contemporary liberal feminism, thus, shared the view that women should be granted equality in society—in law, religion, family, educational system and so on.

Yet another group of feminists and activists that emerged in this phase were women who contended that women would never get equal rights, better facilities, opportunities and an improved status in society till capitalism existed. In 1910, Women's Labor League of Winnipeg was established for bringing economic reforms for women—equal wages for equal work, participation in trade-union movements and better domestic and educational facilities. The abolition of capitalism became the main motive of the Socialist Party of Canada (SPC) who believed that women's freedom could only be attained if the society not only became sex-conscious but also class-conscious. In 1911 Helena Rose Gutteridge organized the BC Women's Suffrage League, after having migrated from London to British Columbia: "to deal with all matters connected with the interests of women, particularly those that affect women in the labour market." (*Ibid.* 34) Socialist activists such as Helena Rose Gutteridge and Edith Wrigley worked for the better working conditions and pay for women. Helena Rose actively participated in the working of the Vancouver Trades and Labour Council. She joined the Federated Labour Party, the Socialist Party of Canada, and then, the Co-operative Commonwealth Federation in 1933.

The contributions of the middle class working women in this endeavour for suffrage and labour conditions are enormous. The year 1895 saw the publication of the first Winnipeg Labour Newspaper *The Voice* and the setting up of the Winnipeg Trades and Labour Council. Equal suffrage was also endorsed by Woman's Labour League in 1910 along with the various efforts of individual activists, trade unionists and other middle class suffrage organizations such as Equal Suffrage Club and the Political Equality League. The period also witnessed the growth of Black women activists who laid down the issues to be taken up by Black feminists in the Second-wave later. Black women and other women of colour who also participated are not widely acclaimed. Organizations such as The Victoria Reform Benevolent Society and the Women's Home Missionary Society of Amherstburg in Ontario and the Coloured Women's Club of Montreal were formed in order to raise funds and assist the black and other women of colour in Canada.

Thus, we see that women who organized and clubbed together followed different philosophies and had varied interests, yet their aim was to unite women to bring reform. At the heart of the women's movement, there was an urge to break free and fight against social ostracism. The First-wave feminists struggled for it all and brought in successful changes. However, it was just the beginning of a well-defined protest against oppression that emerged in the 1960s in Canada, which is referred to as the Second-wave feminism.

Women remained active throughout the years 1920-60 after the First-wave but it was the 1960s that marked the commencement of the Second-wave of feminism. The contemporary women's movement owes its success to their liberation in the 1960s. The Second World War saw the rise of women entering the work force, which made the figure of women in working class to rise from 13% in 1900 to 39% in the 1980s. Married women also began earning and doubling the household income and also witnessed the expansion of educational opportunities for them. More and more female students went to universities and a number of new universities were also founded including Simon Fraser and Tent. Women went to colleges and universities but faced unemployment in the job market. This led to the rise of activism aimed at conscious-raising and improved labour conditions. They also took part in the peace movement and the civil-rights movement in Canada. In 1960 the Voice of Women (VOW) was founded to unite women for the cause of humanity. VOW gradually took up health and safety issues for women and in 1964 it worked for birth control legalization too. The emerging Left parties in Europe and North America influenced the formation of New Left activist groups such as Student Union for Peace Action (SUPA) on many Canadian university campuses.

Family life and traditional notions of sex and marriage began to be challenged. Women no longer feared pregnancy with the availability of the birth control pill in 1966. With the publication of Betty Friedan's *The Feminine Mystique* followed by the appointment of Doris Anderson as editor of *Chatelaine* magazine in 1959 and further the wide circulation of Friedan's book and articles on it, women's movement gained momentum. Divorce laws, reproductive rights and birth control became the issues of women's articles and women's liberation movement. The establishment of the groups such as YWCA, WCTU, the Canadian Federation of University Women, and The National Council for Women, the Business and Professional Women's Clubs and Women's institutions marked changes in the ideological and economic position of women in Canada.

The period 1967-71 indicates the further growth of the women's liberation movement in Canada. Feminists talked about, delivered speeches and discussed issues concerning women. Women formed study circles and read Betty Friedan, Simone de

Beauvoir and Juliet Mitchell. In Montreal, women's emancipation meetings were conducted weekly focusing mainly on abortion rights. Women's caucuses were formed at Simon Fraser University—named Students for a Democratic Union (SDU) which soon became the off-campus Working Women's Association and Vancouver Women's Caucus. In 1968 Toronto Women's Liberation Movement (TWLM) was established along with Vancouver Working Women's Association. A unique aspect of this phase of feminism was CR or consciousness raising campaigns. Eight to ten women gathered and debated and raised the consciousness of other women regarding sex, sexuality, man-woman relationships, abortion laws and friendships and associations among women. Patricia Carey argues in *Canadian Woman Studies*: "the survival and consistent progress [of feminism] can be attributed, I think, to one of its most frequently trivialized symbols and political vehicles: the conscious-raising session." (*Ibid* 44-45) Women began pouring their experiences in feminist magazines and newspapers including *The Pedestal* and *The Velvet Fist*. In 1966 Juliet Mitchell wrote "Women: The Longest Revolution" and in 1967 Judy Bernstein, Peggy Morton, Linda Seese and Myrna Wood—all activists in SUPA—published an article titled "Sisters, Brothers, Lovers Listen" voicing their anger and pain.

One of the major issues of this period was the right to abortion. In 1968 the McGill Student Society published *The Birth Control Handbook* and in 1970 the Vancouver Women's Caucus along with the assistance of Saskatoon Women's Liberation (SWL) group asked women across the entire Canada to join hands in their struggle for birth control rights. The SFU Co-Op Family at Simon Fraser University fought for another important issue—day-care. Day-Care conferences began to be held and became the prior concern of the National Action Committee. Specific issues such as abortion laws and day-care marked the initial stages of the growth of women's organizations and the feminist movement on the whole. The first national conference on women's movement was held in Saskatoon in 1970 on how to focus on specific and general issues. Feminists from various groups separated into different camps in order to promote the efficiency of the work regarding single and multiple issues. For instance, lesbians and radical feminists left the TWLM to form the New Feminists in 1969 and the socialists of Vancouver women's Caucus were expelled from the league to form the Vancouver Women's Alliance.

While grass-roots feminists were out on the streets fighting for their rights, the institutionalized feminists formed more organizations to express their concern for equal human rights. Women formed the Committee for Equality of Women (CEW) which dissolved into the National Ad-hoc Action Committee on the Status of Women (NAC) followed by the Royal Commission on the Status of Women (RCSW). By 1971 NAC had forty two member groups including YWCA, Women's Liberation Movement, National Council for Women, New Feminists, Canadian Federation of University Women, Federated Women's Institute of Canada, Federation of Women Teachers Association of Ontario and so on. By the end of this period, feminists had modified the abortion laws, had formed the RCSW and the first gay liberation group in Canada. The University of Toronto Homophile Association and other organizations and committees had introduced the first Women's Studies course at University of Toronto and published eye-opening articles in feminist newspapers and magazines.

Pamphlets, articles, reviews and research marked this phase of feminism. Early publications including *Women Unite!*, *Century for Struggle, Sisterhood is Powerful* were read and discussed. Theories were being forged regarding the root causes of women's subjugation. A British Columbia activist reported that there were women's groups popping up like popcorn all over the provinces. Women's organizations such as the Canadian Women's Educational Press, The National Association for Women, the Canadian alliance for the Repeal of the Abortion Law (CARAL) along with the B.C. Federation of Women (BCFW) and the Ontario Day-Care Organizing Committee were set up aiming at "a wide range of information for women . . . a referral service to women who are new to the community or who are frightened to approach more specific community services alone; and space where women could meet to share their concerns." (*Ibid.* 55)

Along with grass-roots feminists, lesbians, immigrant women and women of colour also came to the fore to demand their rights. Lesbian feminists had been working with radical feminists but had not come to the limelight. In a speech addressed to an audience of lesbians, on behalf of the Lesbians against the Right (LAR), Lorna Weir defined lesbians as "women whose primary emotional and sexual commitment is to other women. As per the way we live, lesbians claim economic and emotional independence from men. We take the power to explore and discover women's sexuality on women's terms. Lesbians act on women's rights to be with other women, to enjoy the company of women and to organize with women. (*Ibid.* 289)

By supporting lesbians, the women's movement helped women in gaining their right to work and care for other women. The lesbians contend that patriarchy has repressed their sexuality and denied them their identity. They must trace their roots back to Sappho to create their own history. Lesbian feminists had participated in the women's movement earlier as well for issues such as day-care, wages for labour and so on. The first public statement was made at the Indo-Chinese Women's Liberation Conference in Toronto in 1971 during the time when lesbianism had become a potential issue in the American women's movement. In 1972 five lesbians produced and sold the feminist newspaper *The Other Woman* voicing the interests of lesbians. The same year a woman's centre for lesbians, *The Woman's Place*, was also set up holding Friday night Lesbian Drop-Ins for the struggle to maintain a separate identity. In the subsequent year, the first lesbian conference was held in Toronto followed by more Anglophone lesbian conferences in Montreal in 1974 and 1975. Lesbian groups such as *The Lesbian Organization of Toronto* (LOOT) were formed holding concerts, dances, opening coffee houses and so on discussing amendments regarding child sexuality, lesbian rights and so on. Later, *National Lesbian Forum* along with other organizations such as *Woman against Free Trade Committee, Women in Toronto* etc. was also formed. Writers such as Candis J. Graham, Dionee Brand, Sarah Louise, Christina Millis and Carol Camper proved that they have expressed their feelings, suppressed desires and aspirations openly and have succeeded, to a large extent, in asserting their space in society. To put it in Mary Meigs' words, lesbian-feminist writing "is a study of oppression that [is] part of my own experience: suffocation by upper-class principles and squeamishness, the blindness of privilege, the abuse of power by friends, the oppression of enforced heterosexuality." (196)

Another group of women who began to form associations was immigrant women and the women of colour who addressed their issues and struggled to meet their needs and demands. In 1973 a group of Spanish speaking women formed the Centre for Spanish Speaking Peoples (CSSP) in Toronto. In 1974 two significant immigrant women's organizations—Women Working with Immigrant Women (WWIW) and Women's Community Employment Centre (WCEC) were also formed in Toronto concerning labour issues and other job needs. Yet, these were not considered as an integral part of the women's struggle completely. It was only in the 1980s that their positive endeavour was brought to the notice of the people. Immigrant women, black women and other women of colour had been facing confronting racism despite Canada's policy of promoting multiculturalism. They believed that the feminist movement had been a movement dominated by the white women and for the cause of the white women only. In order to express their long-suppressed agony, the women of colour of various backgrounds formed the Visible Minority Women's Coalition in 1983. Women of colour, black, immigrant and native women participated in the events of IWD in 1986. Their contribution to the feminist movement was primarily to incorporate an anti-racist position in the feminist struggle.

The history of the women's movement so far denotes that the emphasis in the 1960s was on the similarities in women—that women constitute one big family and have been victims of repression and oppression in a male-governed society. With the emergence of a large number of women's groups in the 1970s, the focus shifted to the differences. Women are different owing to their caste, race and nationality and have specific problems to tackle. The feminists in the movement broke into small factions thereafter and gave rise to various feminisms—Radical feminism, Liberal feminism, Cultural feminism, Socialist feminism and so on.

In early 1970s, many institutionalized feminists established provincial women councils including Canadian Advisory Council on the Status of Women and the National Action Committee (NAC) and the National Association of Women and the Law. Women were being prepared to speak for themselves in primarily four areas of interest—equal pay, child care, abortion and family property. With the celebration of International Women's Year (IWY) in 1975 in the United Nations, institutionalized feminism received a major boost and women became active in the working of institutions such as the church, trade unions, universities and the medical profession. While the institutionalized feminism aimed at improving the status of women in various institutions and the public sphere, the grass-roots feminism witnessed a political split in 1972 when it broke into chiefly two channels—Radical feminism and Socialist feminism, each with its own agenda and theoretical perspective. At the NAC-organized meeting in 1972, the term 'radical' was used for the first time for all the women who objected to the liberal-democratic system. Radical feminism grew out of the grass-roots feminism in the 1970s and upheld the view that, of all the forms of oppression, women's oppression is the most fundamental, the most severe, and the most difficult to abolish. They believe that the root cause is patriarchy, defined by the renowned radical feminist Zillah Eisenstein as a "sexual system of power in which the male possesses superior power and economic privilege." (Mandell 14) The radical feminists suggested that in order to get rid of this domination patriarchy must be eliminated, and this could be done only if women isolate themselves from "men and from institutions, relationships, roles and activities that are male-defined, male-operated, benefit males and maintain male privilege." (*Ibid.* 14) Women could eradicate this subjugation by creating a woman-identified world, a world of women friendships and lesbian separation. One of the earliest known radical feminists in the history of Canada, Bonnie Kreps, in her article in *Women Unite!* explains the functions of radical feminism as activists who choose "to concentrate exclusively on the oppression of women as *women* and not as workers, students etc. [Radical feminism] therefore concentrates its analysis on institutions like love, marriage, sex, masculinity and femininity. It would be opposed specifically and centrally to sexism rather than capitalism . . . and would not be particularly concerned with 'equal rights' [or] 'equal pay for equal work.'" (Adamson 66)

Radical feminists aimed at liberating women from the so-called 'male values' and posing an alternative culture of women with 'female values.' The idea that women possess these 'female values' or feminine virtues gradually gave way to a more decided moral movement among women—Cultural Feminism. Radical feminist organizations such as Women against Rape in British Columbia and Women against Violence against Women (WAVAW) were formed in Toronto. WAVAW maintained that sex oppression is a universal phenomenon and the eradication of this form of harassment was the most essential—the other divisions of class, race and nationality were mere products of masculine ideology. Out of the radical feminists grew the lesbian feminists who held conferences on the national level and published articles and newspapers propagating their theories and programmes.

Feminists who were socialists had to confront the challenge of consolidating women on issues of class and gender. Socialist feminism had its roots in the socio-political changes of the middle and the late nineteenth century in Western Europe and North America. Whereas the liberal feminists fought for equality of women with men, the socialist feminists considered the changing of the basic structural patterns of society as their immediate goal. They felt that societal structure demarcates categories of gender, race, and class as obstructions to women's emancipation. They stressed on making women realize that they are an integral part of the society who need to rebel against poverty, unequal wages and even unpaid work. They brought to the fore that a capitalist economy propels exploitation of the other and women become the main sufferers as they are financially dependent on their fathers and husbands. The first socialist feminist organization in Canada, the Saskatoon Women's Liberation (SWL) was formed in the 1960s. The group existed till 1981 as one of the longest-lived socialist feminist groups in Canada. The socialist feminist grouped together to understand the concerns of lesbians, immigrant women and women of colour. The need to form allies was strong which led Nancy Adamson, Linda Briskin and Margaret McPhail to come together in the early 1980s in the International Women's Day Committee of Toronto (IWDC). There were other groups functioning such as SWL and Bread and Roses, a Vancouver based socialist feminist group but their efforts were not effective to a great extent. Some trade unionists also formed the Organized Working Women (OWW) for the benefit of all union as well as non-union women. Another organization, Saskatchewan Working Women (SWW) was founded to take up the issues of day-care, familial and working benefits. The grass-roots feminism thus expanded its horizon from mere equal rights to the grouping of women for all their class- and race-based gender problems.

The third group of feminists who consolidated their political power was the Liberal Feminists whose contacts with the media and the government led to the inclusion of a guarantee of equality of women in the Constitution in 1981. The liberal feminists assumed that the ill treatment meted out to women is due to the fact that they have been denied equal rights and have been trained to show their reluctance in demanding them. They advocate social and legal reforms in order to seek equal opportunities and rights for women such as educational opportunities, financial independence and achievement of citizens' rights. In 1970 the Royal Commission on the Status of Women was set up aiming at protection for mothers, employment for married women and special care for the disadvantaged groups of women. In 1984, Abella Report introduced the access to wage labour for women who were married and were of disadvantaged groups.

The rise of the women's movement, the emergence of various feminisms, the contest and protest for equality in all spheres—women in Canada have seen it all. Innumerable organizations, groups and centres have been founded to raise the consciousness as well as the status of women in society. Women have toiled hard to seek a better world of well and justly defined sex roles. Feminists and lesbian-feminists in Canada are therefore moving towards a just social order. Concluding this discussion in the words of Anne Cameron: "whether it is day-care, reproductive rights, equal pay for work of equal value, pornography or racism, we first have to allow hell to burst out, then put things back together again." (Cameron 70)

Canadian Feminist Fantastical Voices

> Child of the pure unclouded brow
> and dreaming eyes of wonder!
> Though time be fleet, and I and thou
> are half a life asunder,
> Thy loving smile will surely hail
> The love-gift of a fairy tale. (Lewis Carroll, 1871)

The German poet Schiller articulates: "deeper meaning resides in the fairy tales told to me in my childhood than in the truth that is taught by life." (Bettelheim 5) The genre of fantasy is made available to young children for the enrichment of socio-cultural values and to propose an alternative human/ non-human world for the cognition of the familiar domain. Fantasy tales are spatio-temporally located differently; rather are not bound by time or space. The child understands that these events took place 'once upon a time,' in perhaps the oldest of times, in distant lands, yet the events are interpreted as taking place in his/ her familiar surroundings. The folk and fairy tales take him/ her through a voyage inside the individual's mind, and so, the encounters that s/he reads or listens to about in the story become his/ her own. At times, the young mind perceives itself to be the valiant hero rescuing the meek princess or the voracious wolf terrorizing the Red Riding Hood. The characters in the tales—human beings/ animals give vent to the child's inner feelings, boost the ego and thereby assist in maturation. By rearranging and fantasizing the events of the narrative, by imagining and day-dreaming, the child discovers new meaning in life. Further, by giving an outlet to his/ her repressed emotions, the requirements of the ego and superego are fulfilled adding new dimension to life itself. Bruno Bettelheim, in an attempt to comprehend the significance of fairy tales, myths and folk tales, writes: "When all the child's wishful thinking gets embodied in a good fairy; all his destructive wishes in an evil witch; all his fears in a voracious wolf; all the demands of his conscience in a wise man encountered on an adventure; all his jealous anger in some animal that picks out the eyes of his archrivals—then the child can finally begin to sort out his contradictory tendencies. Once this starts, the child will be less and less engulfed by unmanageable chaos." (*Ibid.* 66)

The Canadian feminist Gretchen Sankey, in her work on the effect of fairy tales on children, tells us that prior to the seventeenth century, childhood was not even considered a significant phase in the life of an individual. The concept of 'child' was not established till the development in psychological studies which later acknowledged it as the most crucial phase for the growth of an adult human being. As a result, fairy tales, folk tales and myths became popular texts to fulfil its pedagogic needs. Bruno Bettelheim explores the meaning of fairy tales: "fairy tales teach little about the specific conditions of life in modern mass society; these tales were created long before it came into being. But more can be learned from them about the inner problems of human beings, and of the right solutions to their predicaments in any society, than from any other type of story within a child's comprehension." (*Ibid.* 5)

The other genres of literature available to children are fables and myths that work otherwise as compared to the fairy tales. Dr. Samuel Johnson defines a fable as "a narrative in which beings irrational, and sometimes, inanimate, are for the purpose of moral instruction, feigned to act and speak with human interests and passions." (Qtd. *Ibid.* 42-43) A fable normally contains animals—monkeys, wolfs, bears, crocodiles and so on wrought with human emotions and conflicts. The child extrapolates that the animals speak, feel and understand with it, and through the animals' experience, gains knowledge for him/ her. The manifold aspects of an individual's personality are discerned through the reading of fables. The fable is marked by the fabulous; the characters are embodied with human attributes undergoing trials and tribulations. The animals in the fables guide heroes through forests, aid in rescuing captives, mermaids fall in love with humans, frogs turn into princes, the pussy cat and the fox are stereotyped as being wily and cunning respectively. The fables are direct and do not carry any concealed meaning. They state a moral truth: "demand and threaten—they are moralistic—or they just entertain." (*Ibid.* 27)

The authentic rationale of the folk and fairy tales is to provide a plethora of adventures, encounters and vicissitudes for children to enable them to mature while functioning as sources of enhancement and enjoyment. The multiple ends of these tales are put forth by Bettelheim: "Fairy tales, unlike any other form of literature, direct the child to discover his identity and calling, and they also suggest what experiences are needed to develop his character further. Fairy tales intimate that a rewarding, good life is within one's reach despite adversity—but only if one does not shy away from the hazardous struggles without which one can never achieve true identity. These stories promise that if a child dares to engage in this fearsome and taxing search, benevolent powers will come to his aid, and he will succeed. The stories also warn that those who are too timorous down to a humdrum existence—if an even worse fate does not befall them." (*Ibid.* 24)

Myths, on the other hand, are grandiose with uncommon characters or a non-descript 'prince' or 'queen' or even larger than life characters such as Beowulf, Hercules, Theseus or even Adam and Eve. When a child confronts legends laden with myths—biblical or otherwise, it knows that this is not its own story. The child understands that such grand events involving the supernatural intervention—gods and goddesses aiding brave heroes cannot take place around it in reality, but are vital nonetheless to satisfy his/ her superego's demands. The images of the mighty heroes slaying dragons and monsters makes him/ her realize the potential inside and the urge to emulate them. The task of the feminists then is to expose this phallocentrism in the myths and then, using Judith Fetterly's term become the 'Resisting Reader,' in order to invent new symbols, myths and cultural paradigms. (Ramya 1) Jane Caputi extends the submission: "One of the most significant developments to emerge out of the contemporary feminist movement is the quest to reclaim that symbolizing/ naming power to refigure the female self from a gynocentric perspective, to discover, revitalize and create a female oral and visual mythic tradition and use it ultimately to change the world." (425)

Fairy and folk tales are aimed as the stepping stones for laying the foundation for the personality of the individual. They are the social and cultural signifiers embedded in the narratives to be conveyed to the children. Fairy tales, folk tales and myths have been recounted, refined and reinterpreted several times to discover their concealed meanings. The question that arises is that are these stories, simply exportation into the realm of fantasy so as to reflect reality? Through the centuries, fairy tales and fables have been read as a part of children's literature but have formed an important impact on the psychology of adults as well. Western traditional fairy tales have served the precise purpose of transferring cultural values, social codes and mannerisms to people for generations. But what are these social and cultural norms? Are they not the integral essentials of the family system in which we are born and brought up; the patriarchal hegemonic set-up in which we grow up; the society that tutors that the father is the head of the family. Is it not further that since the financial power lays in the hands of the father, he is entitled to lay down the rules and the code of conduct in the family making the mother and the children dependent on him financially as well as emotionally. Noted Canadian writer Elizabeth Vonarburg further alludes to the Bible to polemicize how gender prejudice is a prehistoric notion rooted in religion which has been transmitted to the successive generations. The Bible authenticates that women received their due punishment for eating the forbidden fruit in the form of reproduction of more women, to be treated only as slaves:

> After all, women are inferior here, despite being treated than in the North or the West where they are blamed for the Decline, for consorting with Satan. God has not punished men, but women, women and their progeny. When the time of the Abominations came, says the New Bible, they wanted to take advantage of it, to change their bodies, to be like men. God rightly punished them by condemning them to produce an abundance of daughters—slaves as they themselves became slaves. But the anti-feminist reaction was especially violent in the North and West, where the first wholesale killings took place as Europe fell into social and economic decay. . . . They [women] are slaves. "I said to my *handmaid*, 'Come,' and she came, 'Go,' and she went," says the New Bible. There are no men-servants in this newest Scripture. The very word has vanished. Women are objects to be manipulated at will. (Vonarburg 77)

In her essay "When the Goods Get Together," Luce Irigaray refers to women as 'goods' or 'commodities' which are traded and exchanged in a patriarchal society. The man buys and another man pays for the transaction of marriage to take place. So, it is a transaction of money and phallic power between two men and never between women. Women are objects of male desire who pass from one man to another and relapse into the system and Irigaray reads this relapse as a penalty. The woman of the house becomes subordinate; she is labelled as the 'inferior sex.' She is confined to her domestic space performing her household chores with humility and dexterity. She learns submission and servility towards the bread earner of the family. She is the Annapurna and ought to cook delicious food, produce and rear children perfecting the art with compliance. When she is young, she imbibes gender stereotypes of obedience, self-abnegation and obsequiousness. The performance of the ascribed role is carried out throughout lifetime as daughter, wives and mothers.

The coercive forces of patriarchy, resulting in the domination and abuse of women, have formed the subject matter of women's literature time and again. Female writers have accentuated the marginalization of the so-called 'weaker sex' in their literature. Writers either posited the state of women but left things unsaid or utilized their writing as a potent tool to express the pent up anger against this oppression. In the twentieth century, women writers took up the task of "phallic criticism," as Mary Ellman puts it, to expose the sexist criticism in literature. They decided to write—to write stories in which women seek their individuality. Shirin Kudchedkar writes in "Feminist Voices from India and Canada": "Western feminist writers (and Western has hitherto meant White Canadian, American or European writers) are concerned with a woman's or girl's encounter with the world, her efforts to define herself, to find viable ways of living." (2)

Feminism, as a movement in Canada, aims at exposing the politics of the clichéd projections of women in literature. The canonical and the non-canonical—novels, plays, poems and other genres along with the fairy tales, myths and folklore—have served as a medium to transmit the cultural beliefs on to children, in order that they are permeated and rooted in the subconscious and conscious self. If the messages conveyed are opinionated, the repercussions would be highly harmful. A child listens/reads to these stories with a promise of refinement, but these tales "cheat the child of what he ought to gain from the experience of literature: access to deeper meaning, and which is meaningful to him at this stage of development." (Bettelheim 4)

Women's studies, thus, analyze how these narratives have depicted woman as the timid object of male gaze and the consequential transmission of the dominant power structures of patriarchy. Traditional tales have been operational in setting these cultural constructs directly or vicariously. In the Introduction to *Room of One's Own: A Space for Women's Writing*, the noted Canadian feminist writer Wendy Putman states:

> I am still fascinated by the messages filtered to our collective subconscious through traditional tales. These stories have a tremendous impact on the way we, as women, are trained to perceive the world. The way we learn to speak—by listening, mimicking, and setting down communication patterns in our minds, so do we absorb the constructions prescribing gender assigned roles and proscribing social scripts at a highly impressionable stage of our development. The structures of traditional tales are reinforced all around us, from the paradigms to the hierarchies of business to popular culture. (1)

Women in conventional tales are marked for their beauty, youth and innocence. They are the passive maidens who have no will of their own and are incapable of thinking rationally for themselves. The narratives project them as inferior to men and having accepted patriarchal hegemony. In her efforts at defining the role of women in these tales and the subsequent effects on the readers, Kaarina Kailo tells us that women are shown as the meek sisters who serve as hand-maidens to men—from dwarves to princes or young princesses waiting earnestly for their princes, savior and lord to come and rescue them from the clutches of the diabolical beasts. The male heroes or princes derive pleasure in gazing at their female object of desire and conquering them and thereby satisfying their ego. She writes: "Even when women seemingly occupy centrestage as the main characters of Western fairy tales, these stories simply reproduce Christian, mainstream, patriarchal fantasies about proper female behavior. The typical polarized models of femininity that girls end up internalizing as the good/ bad gender-specific modes of behavior are equally empowering for them. Folktale 'heroines' . . . remain locked in their need for protection, rescue and romanticized heterosexual dependency." (Kailo 87)

Feminist writers in Canada have therefore taken up the task of retelling these myths and tales to assert their vision of a land of promised equality. Kaarina Kailo points out that rewriting fairy tales and myths help women writers "to interact with . . . internalized images of femininity and to play-act with characters in . . . [their] inner theatre," and it is their duty "to go through these stages of deconstruction (taking our traditions and cultures apart so as to see what makes them tick) and the stage of reconstructions, re-visioning, re-appropriation." (*Ibid*. 91)

The project of rewriting the established tales begins with the prime myth—the myth of creation. The Fall of Man or the original sin has been religiously attributed to Eve. According to Genesis, the biblical story of creation, Lilith, the prototype of Eve was created before Eve as man's equal. When she was denied her sexual authority she fled in quest of her freedom. Hence, Lilith is mythicized culturally as a sexual she-beast who is untamed and whose sexuality is unveiled for all to glare at. God then created Eve as subordinate to Adam/ Man and the former tasted the forbidden fruit succumbing to Satan's temptations. The biblical story renders Eve as a seductive temptress whose association with the serpent led to the cognizance of her sexuality and brought anarchy to man's blissful state. So culture mythifies man as the innocent victim and the woman as the seductress. Women's sexuality is thus linked to Satan—the originator of evil in the world. Hence, her sexuality must be repressed and not given a chance to unleash or else she would become bestial and uncontrollable like Lilith. For this reason, man needs to maintain that whenever a woman expresses her sexual desires she is actually exhibiting masculine traits since sexuality is his tool of power. Her sexual assertion can only bring chaos to mankind so she needs to be submissive, subdued and compliant for the betterment of the entire human race.

Hence, all of Eve's daughters, who have asserted their sexuality, have been characterized as dangerous. In the words of Tamara Steinborn: "A close analysis of our culture shows how the true daughters of Eve, all womankind, have been myth-laden to a negative extreme. . . . Woman, as virago, has become dangerous, overpowering, and sexually threatening to man in his world of reason and order." (35) Milton describes the classical image of Eve:

> Eve: "But to Adam in what sort
> Shall I appear? . . .
> But keep the odds of Knowledge in my power
> in Female Sex, the more to draw his love,
> and render me more equal, and perhaps
> a thing not undesirable. (John Milton, *Paradise Lost*)

The text clearly typifies that the evil in Eve or woman is closely associated with her sexuality. In order to de-mythify the archetypal image of Eve, Virginia Lee Hines presents two different interpretations of the 'Eve' story in her poem "An Old Story." In its first section, the poet describes how Eve, "Motherless," became the mother of all the women on Earth, and thus, initiated her daughters into sin—the sin of the expression of their sexual urges. Eve's original behaviour in the garden became the "thorny grove" for all women. She imbued women with their feminine body parts, "certain breasts, womb soft skin," along with a craving to break free from the clutches of repressed sexuality. The poem is a reminiscence of William Blake's *Songs of Innocence and Experience*. She writes:

Oh, I feel now
how she felt confined to Eden, naked,
so innocent longing for sin.
Let me set down my cup of cocoa,
grab my coat, my purse,
run from ordered house,
take chances in unknown territory. (Lee Hines 33-34)

In the second part of the poem, Eve is emblematic of the modern woman caught in the web of penury, "cooking oatmeal mornings on an undependable gas burner" with no one to count on in an urban materialistic world, ever struggling for survival and identity. Instead of showing Eve lurking in the dark shadows of lust and eroticism, it is Adam, with his "brash craziness" and "uncertain temperament" that encroaches upon her world. Adam yearns to fulfil his carnal appetite and ego by conquering her in the sexual act:

intrudes
into my wanderings, calling my name.
He lusts for me, the reluctant
twin. We roll into each other
bruising our skins, our egos,
then fly apart.

Eve's or the woman's body succumbs to male passion and the original garden turns her body into a garden where Adam wanders into to pluck her whenever he wills to do so:

her body yielding to passion, birth—
woman becomes a garden.

Virginia Lee Hines, thus, breaks the traditional notion of Eve as the original enchantress along with her daughters as evil or the 'mad women in the attic' to borrow Sandra Gilbert and Susan Gubar's phraseology. The retelling of the myth articulates the silenced—the plight of women as objects of male gaze and erotic desire.

One of the conventional fairy tale plots consists of a young prince falling in love with a poor girl followed by their marriage as consummation of their love. So the poor girl gets to marry a rich handsome prince and lives happily ever after. The young girl is illustrated as a paragon of beauty, innocence, docility and femininity. The prince ought to be the brave gallant riding on horses, fighting dragons and monsters, and, in short, the epitome of masculinity. This fairy tale heroine must preserve her beauty and chastity till the prince comes to claim it in due time. She has to make the right choice—to exist for the prince, take care of their children and so on. What else could she ask for? Such is the case with the heroine of our story, Cinderella. Having waited for years for some miracle to take place, Cinderella meets her prince at the ball with the help of her fairy godmother. The prince is bewitched, falls in love, marries Cinderella and the fairy tale ends on a happy note.

What happened after the prince married Cinderella? Elizabeth Greene gives us a sequel to the tale in a different tone and a not-so-happy ending. Greene's fairy tale, "Cinderella's Daughters" does not begin conventionally 'once upon a time.' It opens fifteen or twenty years after the marriage of Cinderella with her prince. The original fairy tale heroine has not altered a bit. She is the same Cinderella, who was "sweet and good in the face of the wicked stepmother and stepsisters" (Greene 60-65), likes romances and picture books, and "only cared about running the house and taking care of people and gardens and helping the poor." However, in Greene's narrative, Cinderella's daughters Annabelinda and Zoe, who were lovely and intellectual when they were born, do not turn into the typecast heroines. The first disappointment comes when the reader is told that they are not beautiful. Annabelinda has sallow thin shoulders and Zoe is overweight with bad skin. When they play house, they cook stories of "bloodcurdling adventures and escapes." In place of boys, it is the female dolls that slay the dragons and rescue others. In total defiance of the cultural norms, the girls are rude and moody and "unprincesslike" who prefer to stay gloomy and morose rather than being cheerful and bright in public. To the mother's amazement, Annabelinda reads historical novels at the age of ten while Zoe reads poetry which her mother fails to understand. The sisters even discuss their bodies, desires and embarrassments furtively. Annabelinda has only girlfriends and Zoe goes out only with boys. The former writes refined film and play reviews while the latter produces luxuriant poems and spiteful journals. Cinderella's agony is described thus: "Cinderella began to get headaches and bad bouts of bronchitis. . . . Her daughters should be growing into beauty, but every day took them further from feminine perfection. What prince would look at them? How would they make their way in the world? How would they find happy endings?"

The twist in this story, as in the original one, comes with the entry of the fairy godmother. The prince invites the fairy godmother to come and stay with them to restore the chaotic order. Cinderella's agony is put to rest as the fairy godmother tells the sisters: "you are each the heroines of your own lives, and you will find your own transformations. Your mother will understand that."

The reader may expect that the godmother is successful in transforming the sisters who eventually meet their princes, get married, and live happily ever after. But the author has a different story to tell. For Annabelinda: "heterosexual romantic love remained a closed book" and "she did meet a woman she loved." She begins to teach and write, and in time, becomes a renowned feminist. Since she has an archetype for a mother, she tries: "not to write too harshly of women who made conventional choices." Greene depicts Zoe's fate thus: "Zoe herself, torn between example of mother and sister, went to graduate school, got a job, fell in love, got pregnant, miscarried, married and had children in that order. She couldn't help being grateful for her husband's affections, and the power shifted in their relationship so that she was always trying to please him and he was always asking for more."

Zoe finally ends her marriage and recuperates the wounds of an unhappy wedded life. She takes care of her children, falls in love again, but does not marry again. She begins to write meaningful poetry and becomes a successful writer too. Cinderella accepts her daughter's choices gradually and adores her successive generations.

Elizabeth Greene's reshaping of the Cinderella story problematizes the objectification of women and the need to change the accepted patterns of dominant patriarchy. In Greene's fairy tale, men do not have much role to play. The prince has no masculine prowess to display; the daughters do not meet their princes. The female protagonists challenge the sweet, pretty, submissive stereotype. The fairy godmother does not advise the girls to follow the conventions. The sister who makes the conformist choice ends up with a broken marriage and a bruised heart. It is only when the two sisters resolve to live and grow independently that the author finally provides them with a happy ending. Greene closes the narrative with the words: "There are other stories of Cinderella's daughters. Probably you know some yourself. But these are the two I choose to tell."

In order to present how women have been 'pickled' for the male gaze, Kaarina Kailo, re-interprets the fairy tale of "The Snow White." Like Cinderella, the Snow White also incorporates the myth of the beautiful princess craving for the "waited-for-prince." She is as white as snow, needs to starve herself in a coffin, to stay "eternally young, skinny, beautiful, desirable, rescue-worthy" (Kailo 89). She is the ideal woman, perfect in beauty and worth, 'pickled' and 'preserved' for the male gaze of the prince who will kiss her to make her immortal. Kailo's student, Caroline Desbiens-Magalios expresses the Snow White syndrome: "Snow White is the ideal woman once preserved under the glass coffin: passive, virginal, sublimely beautiful and deliciously sensual, like the forbidden fruit. She becomes the apple herself which the prince will pick and taste without fear of punishment, for the standard is different: arousal of the erotic power constitutes a woman's fall but a man's elevation." (*Ibid.*)

Similarly "Red Riding Hood" is also associated with the propagation of females with a sexual passivity and dependence on men. The Little Red Riding Hood has to deliver some delicacies to her grandmother who stays in a cottage in the forest. Her mother forbids her not to go through the woods and to take the longer route fearing the wolf could devour the little girl. The Red Riding Hood promises to obey her mother but gets tempted to take the short cut through the woods. The wolf however notices her and eats both the Red Riding Hood and her grandmother eventually.

In "Re-viewing the Life and Times of Little Red Riding Hood," Gretchen Sankey explains that the story is not just a simple fairy tale, but an attempt at the dissemination of the tenets of sexual passivity and self-abnegation in women. The wolf in the story is the "predatorial man, inclined to seduce if given the slightest chance" (Sankey 53). The mother prohibits the Riding Hood from going into the woods for fear of the wolf who would ravish her. The Red Riding Hood's decision to explore the forbidden territories is equated with her violent sexual emotions, also associated with her red cap, the colour red being associated with danger as well as passion. Since the little girl gives in to her innocuous desires, she has to pay the price and has to bear the burden of guilt of the sexual abuse for having chosen the unsafe route herself. The fairy tale distinctly admonishes little girls from defying the said norms. Jack Zipes disputes that the writers of fairy tales "were men who were interested in preserving patriarchal norms, and therefore, Little Red Riding Hood's image must be seen as a male creation and projection," and that the widespread and friendly reception of the fairy tale owes to the "general acceptance of the cultural notions of sexuality, sex roles and domination embedded in it" (Qtd. *Ibid.* 54). In *Building Babel* Suniti Namjoshi creates a wonderful encounter of the Red Riding Hood with the wolf. The girl is smart enough to trick the wolf this time by telling him that he is not just a wolf but also a man:

> "So what?" says the wolf.
> "Marry me!"
> "What good would that do?"
> "Then we'll have kids and farm the land."
> "Have you got any land?"
> "Yes," replied Red. "But I've got to clear it of wolves first. I need your help." (*Building Babel* 24)

Another of the 'pickled' heroines in fairy tales is "The Little Mermaid." The Little Mermaid is the loveliest and prettiest of all her sisters. The story tells us: "all the Mer-princesses were extremely beautiful, but the little mermaid, who was the youngest, had the prettiest hair . . . and the bluest eyes" (Anderson 191). The Little Mermaid is not allowed to leave the coral palace and swim freely in the blue sea as per the Mer-king's law. However, when she turns fifteen, she is permitted to go above the sea where she rescues a handsome prince from drowning in the storm and falls in love with him. In order to win his love, she appeals to the sea-witch to get rid of her tail and have a pair of legs in its place. The witch agrees to do so in exchange of the mermaid's melodious voice. The mermaid turns speechless and goes to the prince's palace but is not fortunate enough to get reciprocation of her love and so finally retreats.

What is the message of this fairy tale? At first, the Little Mermaid is forbidden to violate or question her father's law. Being a clichéd fairy tale, the female protagonist's only aim is to win the prince's love and get married to him. Kaarina Kailo elucidates: "True to this fixated frozen image, girls are conditioned with the dominant fairy tales in the Western hemisphere to pickle themselves, to repress their orality, to hold their tongues and to internalize the sexual dogmas uncritically. The Little Mermaid is the arch-representative of the woman who is willing to give up speech, self-expression, language in order to 'get' her prince." (Kailo 88)

Such models of self-effacement are abundantly prevalent in Western fairy tales to propagate the Christian concepts of self-sacrifice and humility in women. The only fulfillment a woman can seek is in finding her companion, who will aid her in reaching her womanhood, give birth to his children and live happily ever after.

Pauline Rankin reworks the Mermaid tale in her story titled "A Mermaid Tail." The author opens her narrative with the declaration: "THIS IS NO WIDE-EYED cartoon story," emphatically stating that the reader must not expect it to be the usual fairy tale. The Little Mermaid of this story is a powerful and determined swimmer who swims through murkier waters, strange places and colder seas to look for her companion. There is no Mer-king and no forbidden law to establish the negation of patriarchy and its edicts straightaway. Outside the realm of the patriarchal structure, the mermaid is free to swim above the seas and explore the unfamiliar territories. The mermaid finally reaches a land house where, instead of meeting her prince, she meets a woman: "There she saw the most beautiful woman walking along the shore, on sturdy and powerful legs. The mermaid hauled herself out of the water, where she lay half fainting with exertion and delight. The land-woman hurried to her side. . . . She almost fainted with delight, as well." (Rankin 42-43)

The mermaid and the land-woman begin to visit each other frequently—one day on the land and the other day on the sea. The two gradually fall in love with each other and make love to each other. In opposition to the original mermaid story, the mermaid does not have to forfeit her tail or voice for gaining the love of her companion. The author writes: "the land-woman spoke in human tones. The mermaid sounded her dolphin voice. They did not miss the words."

In a male-governed story, the mermaid loses her identity fully. Earlier, it is the father who lays down the rules and later, it is the prince whose love forces her to forego her selfhood. Once she is out of this domination, she is free to choose her partner, who need not be a man anymore. Neither of the two women ought to sacrifice their individuality. The mermaid feels that she does not want to give up her potent swimming tail and the land-woman wishes not to lose her strong legs. The writer renders a solution: "they decided to continue as they were: sometimes in land, sometimes in water." In this manner, the duo stayed together by lending each other enough space for themselves, which is denied in patriarchy. In the re-writing of the tale, Pauline Rankin, therefore, brings to light the repression of women and offers the reader an alternative matriarchal society in which women need not deprive themselves of their emotional or sexual desires. There is complete absence of male characters in the story to authenticate the feminist writer's assertion that women's happiness does not necessarily lay with heterosexuality in addition to the fact that lesbian relations are equally promising. Noted lesbian feminist critics Alice, Gordon, Debbie and Mary underscore: "Lesbians, by loving women and not men, pose a direct threat to the very basis of male supremacy. From this analysis, we conclude that lesbians have the ability and commitment to women that will be necessary to overthrow male supremacy and its attendant forms of oppression." (Qtd. Andermahr 134)

While presenting the paradigmatic difference between the traditional and the tales retold by women, Carolina Fernández Rodríguez writes: "The former group of texts are responsible for the inscription of the male rescuer archetype; in other words, they constitute a well-known corpus of tales where the rescuing agent is constantly presented as a male, thus conveying the idea that the redeemer is naturally a man. As opposed to this, feminist revisions attempt to demythologize the traditional hero, and, on the other hand, to offer different alternatives to it. In this way they prove that not all male figures are competent rescuers and also that female figures can sometimes perform the rescuing function more remarkably." (52)

The male sovereignty is also endorsed in the famous "Rapunzel"—a tale of a couple who steal a handful of rampion from a witch's garden and have to pay the price by giving their loveable daughter, Rapunzel, to the witch. Rapunzel is locked in a castle and is forbidden to step outside. Whenever the witch has to climb the tower to reach Rapunzel's room she utters: "Rapunzel, Rapunzel, let down your golden hair" and uses her long thick tresses as a ladder. One day, a prince riding by hears Rapunzel's melodious voice and gets enchanted by it. He gets to know the witch's secret and cries: "Rapunzel, Rapunzel, let down your golden hair." He uses her hair as a staircase to reach the top. The young girl feels that the prince would love her more and plans to escape with him. The narrative that follows is the witch's finding out their plan of elopement, planting Rapunzel in a remote desert, the prince turning blind followed by meeting his beloved finally, getting his eyesight back and their staying happy ever after. At the outset, the fairy tale is a regular story of a prince rescuing a young girl entrapped by a wicked witch. Nonetheless, one cannot ignore the gendered values embedded in it. The tale, once again, exemplifies women as compliant and cowardly waiting for their princes to come and rescue them. 'Pickled' and 'Preserved' for the prince to come, Rapunzel sings in her solitude and is dumb to the extent of not ever planning to escape herself. The account reports that the protagonist had never seen a man in her life and yet she feels that she would be happier with the prince and not the witch! Such stories and such heroines are consciously constructed for the sustentation of the patriarchal order that validates the fact that only a man can provide physical as well as emotional security to a woman. The female protagonist carries the cultural paradigms of beauty and dependency while the male protagonist conveys the virtues of valour and independence. Kaarina Kailo points out once again in this respect: "girls are encouraged to put the lid on their self-development, while life is an open field, an open season for the self-expanding boys" (89), so true, in the case of Rapunzel.

A twist of perception is palpable in the Rapunzel story in Melissa Branicky's poem "Rapunzel, Rapunzel, let down your hair." The poem offers a substitute to the young damsel who gets lured by the prince in hope of fulfillment of emotional and sexual desires. Like Rapunzel, every woman gives in to her desires and lets down her hair. Like the prince, every man uses a woman's beauty as a staircase to reach the top. He entices her by praising her looks but his real motive is to satisfy his physical needs only. The poet writes:

> Like Rapunzel,
> every time a man calls out to you,
> you throw him down
> your long thick hair,
> slowly each of them has climbed,
> groping his way up your back,
> tangling your beauty into a ladder. (Branicky 50-51)

Slowly, the man empowers the woman completely with the pretext of making love to her. The woman's body begins an ache but she is acquiescent with the illusion that the man is fulfilling her needs:

> All the while
> Your neck strains,
> the flesh itching
> with the ache
> you constantly mistake for desire.

The poet pleads Rapunzel and all the women to understand that the man in her life is no prince but an ordinary mortal who hurts her physically and mentally by displaying his superiority over her in the sexual act and otherwise. Each time Rapunzel is wounded, she comes to the aid of the poet to recuperate:

> So you come to me,
> And I kiss your bruises,
> But I can never make you realize,
> He has yet to be a prince.

The poet offers an alternative to Rapunzel—to cut her hair permanently so that no prince can injure by climbing over her. The poet, thus, advises women to break free from heteronormative bondage and to further seek alternative modes of happiness:

> Let me wield my shears
> and free you from these burdens.
> I can no longer bear to watch you
> supporting this kind of weight.

Canadian feminist writers have also focused on short fables and stories to strengthen the vision of a utopian land where women will enjoy the same rights and privileges as men do. In order to illustrate this, one can look at "Plucking" by Lorna Schwenk and "Tree and Bear" by Frances Rooney. The formal fable demonstrates the woman's agony of being used and discarded emotionally and physically by the man. "Plucking" is the story of two birds of opposite sexes and the various stages of their relationship. The narrative unfolds with the she-bird entering the life of the he-bird who is stupefied by the former's looks. The he-bird next seeks permission to pluck one of her feathers. The courtship begins and the female bird blossoms in love. The wooing ceases but the he-bird continues to pluck more of her feathers without even asking her. The she-bird begins to wither as her feathers are plucked and splotches of white skin begin to appear: "The plucking continued, however, late at night when she was defenceless and tired, or at a weak moment when she needed him the most." (Schwenk 31-32) The plucking further continued till one day she realized that not a single feather was left on her body: "she was completely bare. Not a feather left. Nothing. She was a bald, pale, naked, embarrassed bird. Didn't even *look* a bird anymore."

The she-bird searches her house for her feathers and finds some in his ashtray, some in the dust, some caked and dried, and some in the basement with worn socks and broken shoes. The bird is hurt at finding how her feathers had been used by her companion. The story ends with the bird's realization that she has been exploited by him and her wait for her feathers to grow back on her body. And the author tells us, that each time, it took a long time to heal her wounds, indicating that it was an ongoing process: "He called her later that day to say he didn't need her anymore, so she went off to recuperate and wait for her feathers to grow back, but it took a long time. It always did."

Symbolically, a bird is associated with freedom and flight yet the writer portrays the bird as helpless and clinging to the opposite sex for support in order to bring out the irony. Plucking, therefore, serves her as a metaphor for the sexual exploitation of the female sex and the loss of feathers signifies her loss of identity. The writer does not state the moral but leaves it for the reader to interpret. She implicitly hints that women unknowingly submit to men as the system coerces them to do so. The writer, through the fable, raises her voice against this sexual oppression with an advice for women to desist from heterosexual enslavement.

If Lorna Schwenk registers her protest vicariously, Frances Rooney tells a fabulous tale where the feminist writer's claim is apparent. "Tree and Bear" is situated in a verdant forest where the flora and fauna coexist happily. A curse befalls on the forest due to which there is complete destruction. All the living creatures perish and when light is restored after a period of complete darkness, no life is left, except in a half-grown sapling. The soil in which the little Tree stood is poisonous and so the poor Tree awaits her death. When the Tree opens her eyes, she sees that a small Bear is clinging onto her trunk. The Bear tells her that everything has been devastated and that they should leave the place at once. The Tree believes that this is not possible and tells the Bear: "I can't. I can't move. This is where I started to grow, and if I cannot grow here, I must die here. That is the law for Trees. . . . I am dead already. I just don't know it yet because there are still leaves on my branches, and my bark has not turned to charcoal. My life is over, Bear. That is hard, but it is true." (Rooney 33-37)

The Bear tries hard to persuade the Tree but to no avail. The Tree advocates that if she endeavours to uproot herself she would get hurt and bruised, for no Tree has ever dared to take such a step! Trees are supposed to grow and die at their fixed places. The Tree says: "no Tree has ever walked in the whole back time of earth. Never, never, never, it can't be done." The spirit of Hope reads the Tree's mind and appears in order to impart some of her 'self' to the Tree. She assures the Tree that although it is extremely difficult to relocate oneself, yet struggling to live is more promising than waiting to die. Hope comforts the

Tree: "Your heart will not break, dear Tree. It has broken already. Now it is healing. The pain you feel is the pain of life, of being alive, of becoming and growing strong, and seeing what you must do, and being afraid, and not holding back in fear. Your heart will not break again, Tree, not the way it has. It will never again feel the pain it has felt. That I promise you, Tree."

The Tree agrees to accompany the Bear and with great effort and pain pulls her roots out of the earth. Her branch breaks and her back is torn, yet with Hope in heart she advances with the Bear. The Bear kisses her roots and throughout the night aids her in learning to walk. Both of them become strong and happy towards their journey: "towards other animals for Bear to run with, toward other Trees for Tree to intertwine her branches with, and toward rich and nourishing soil to feed Tree's bruised roots and trunk and branches and leaves."

The Tree in the fable connotes the woman who has lost everything on account of some tragedy and does not have the courage to stand in the face of adversity. The fact that women have been tutored since childhood to be reliant on their fathers and husbands makes them so vulnerable that they begin to believe that moving out of their confined space is next to impossible—the law for trees as the story tells us. Women do have a choice: either they can remain in their defined roles and suffer and die or strive towards a better life even if that is possible only at the cost of defying the patriarchal norms. The Bear becomes the spokesperson of the writer, who lends to the reader, the moral of the fable: "Tree, I know it's impossible. I know it's never been done. I know you can't. . . . You can either stay here or do what's ordinary and tree-like and possible, or you can do the extraordinary and the impossible and leave here. You can stay and die, or you can go and live. There are no other choices."

Thus, one sees how fairy tales, folklore, myths and fables have been political carriers of social and cultural codes. These narratives are not simply material forming bedtime stories but a conscious technique to ingrain gendered values in children. By re-writing these stories, Canadian feminist writers have made a sincere effort in making women conscious of their unconscious submission to men and making them rise out of this slumber. They have broken the conventional notions of women passed on to generations and have created new models for women to emulate. To conclude with the words of Kaarina Kailo: "By rewriting the very stories that controlled us in so many ways, we can finally have our cake and eat it too. We can kiss ourselves awake from the hundreds of years of fruitful waiting, the miracles that don't happen, the rescuers that more often than not leave women in the lurch. Stories have the power to reawaken our senses, in all the senses of the word. Stories are . . . our gynocentric wonderlands. They promise hope and healing if we take the time to reconsider the values we transmit through them to children, if we take the time to UN-think." (92)

Suniti Namjoshi's Theory of Lesbian Feminism

She writes to make a name for herself
Then loses it in the writing
Forges an image that throws her out of herself
To fill the hiatus between extremes of loving
Dons a mask of a woman
To prove that's what she is
What does a woman want?
The question asks too little. (Lola Lemire Tostevin 1997)

The question asks too little and yet too much for a woman writer set on a task to explore the very dilemma of being a woman. It becomes the central concern in the works—criticism, fiction, poetry and theory—of almost every woman writer or feminist. Introducing Suniti Namjoshi in the light of the above statement would be fair enough as her works are devoted to the exploration of the female condition. Namjoshi's works mark a voyage into the female psyche and unearth its various facets. "Gifted with the unique capacity for ironic perception," (Chavan 78) Suniti Namjoshi's profile as a poet, a fabulist and a fiction writer has made her popular, and yet, not so popular owing to her 'Asian' and 'lesbian' identity. Her recognition as a writer of the Indian Diaspora settled in Britain is deliberately reduced as she outrageously claims to be a lesbian and advocates a lesbian utopic vision in her works. In *Because of India* Suniti discusses this problematics of identity of a woman refusing to accept categories—diasporic and heterosexual:

> Identity isn't only a matter of self-definition. It also depends on the identity that other people attribute to one. . . . As a creature, a les-

> bian creature, how do I deal with all the other creatures who have their own identities, or perhaps I mean their own identifications? It's apparent that the components of the core identity change from place to place and period to period. Today the main components seem to be based on gender, skin colour, and sexual choice, as well as other factors such as nationality and religion. . . . Any threat to the sense of self causes a violent reaction. But then how are we all to live? (*Because of India* 84)

This is evident from the fact that her name is omitted or scantly mentioned in most of the accounts of Indian Writing in English or anthologies of critical essays like *Indian Women Novelists*, *The World Within: A Study of Novels in English of Indian Women 1950-1980*, *Recent Indian Fiction* or *Glimpses of Indo-English Fiction* as pointed out by Ananya Dasgupta. This is ironical as her first volume was published by the Writers' Workshop, Calcutta.

Suniti Namjoshi has published numerous poems, fables, articles and reviews in India, Canada, United States and Britain. From her first volume of poetry *Poems* published in 1967 in India to her latest work *Foxy Aesop aka Aesop the Fox* in 2018, Namjoshi has fused diverse genres—of poetry, fiction, fable and myth to sketch out her theory of lesbian feminism. She does not share a literary ancestry or milieu with writers like R.K. Narayan, Amitav Ghosh or Mulk Raj Anand or a distinct style with other Indian women writers in English such as Anita Desai, Nayantara Sahgal or Ruth Prawer Jhabvala. Her style—scandalous and shocking—might even baffle the Indian reader who has accustomed himself/ herself to reading the unconventional poetry of Kamala Das. Her writing is unique in its own way—set apart from the nostalgic, past-retrieving experiences of her contemporary diasporic associates such as Rohinton Mistry, Bharati Mukherjee and M.G. Vassanji. A sharp wit and ironical sensibility define her style, which is truly Indian, although she refuses to describe her life in India in detail in her works. Her postcolonial diasporic location empowers her to state the case of women who are marginalized at multiple levels. Her position is allied to the stance taken up by the Indo-Briton film maker Pratibha Parmar in relation to lesbians and gays of colour:

> We are not interested in defining ourselves in relation to someone else or something else, nor are we simply articulating our cultural and sexual differences. . . . We are creating a sense of ourselves and our place within different and sometimes contradictory communities, not simply in relation to . . . not in opposition to . . . nor in reversal to . . . nor as a corrective to . . . but in and for ourselves. Precisely because of our lived experiences of racism and homophobia, we locate ourselves not within any one community but in the spaces between these different communities. (Qtd. Mann 101)

Suniti Namjoshi's style of poetry is succinctly rhythmic and far from superfluity. A few of Namjoshi's poems illustrate this fraught situation such as "The Old Country" in *More Poems:*

> The old country says
> my young people are all out,
> voyaging through strange lands.
> and the old country says
> to these strange new lands,
> look at my young people.
> Have I not brought them up well?
> look at the shape of their eyes
> and the colour of their skin.
> My minerals fed them.
> and now they are all out
> and home ground well.

In "Emigree" in *The Jackass and the Lady*, she laments again: "in my own country I was a princess," "Yes, but this is not your own country, miss. . . . We are all princes in exile, she sang, picking seashells, clamshells, crayfish and crabs." The thought reverberates in her poem "How to be a Foreigner" in *More Poems*:

> First,
> you take off your clothes,
> your titles and name
> and put on a robe,
> sterile and clean,
> with neat black letters,
> marking THE STRANGER
> then,
> you walk down the street,
> alone in fancy dress.

Ironically true, but it is Namjoshi's Indian and lesbian identity that is at the core of all her works. Her fusion of the various genres is symbolic of the fusion of her Indianness with her so-called Western lesbian identity. It is these categories that she constructs and deconstructs adapting a self-reflexive mode to find out the relation of the individual with the world, the self versus the other. However, the oscillation between the Indian and Western culture is reflected in some of her earlier poems. Ruth Vanita admires her as a poet "to be at home in more than one land and to write about several cultures as insiders." It is the lesbian mindset that dominates her writings till she eventually envisages it in the form of a matriarchal utopia—a final displacement into an all women alien space where neither patriarchy nor diasporic migration shall be a cause of distress. In the subsequent analysis, we shall, however, expose how 'lesbianism' has its roots in the Indian culture centuries ago. For this purpose, she uses witches, monsters, princes, birds and beasts in her fables and myths positioning every one as the "other" and yet identifying with them as one. "All right, I was a beast, a creature. But what sort of beast was I?" She further says:

> To me a beast wasn't "bestial" in the Western sense. To me a bird or a beast was a creature like anyone else. Hinduism is, after all, pantheistic; and the popular notion of reincarnation attributes a soul to everyone. This may sound odd to Western ears, but for me, it was familiar as it was unconscious. . . . It's apparent to many women that in a humanist universe, which has been male-centred historically, women are "the other," together with the birds and the beasts and the rest of creation . . . but I don't want to be separated from the birds and the beasts, nor do I want to "humanize" them particularly. (*Because of India* 28-29)

The first reactions to Suniti Namjoshi's works would be that they are unconventional, immoral and outrageous. Harveen S. Mann corroborates this: "Identity isn't only a matter of self-definition. It also depends on the identity that other people attribute to one. . . . As a creature, a lesbian creature, how do I deal with all the other creatures who have their own identities, or perhaps I mean their own identifications? It's apparent that the components of the core identity change from place to place and period to period. Today the main components seem to be based on gender, skin colour, and sexual choice, as well as other factors such as nationality and religion. . . . Any threat to the sense of self causes a violent reaction. But then how are we dominant Western gay and lesbian theory?" (Mann 98) A closer analysis reveals that whereas fairy and folk tales are supposed to be carriers of cultural norms, Namjoshi's tales subvert and invert the laid social order. Namjoshi's prime concern in re-telling of the fairy tales and fables is to reject all forms of authority and stereotypical notions of women depicted in them and also to offer alternate visions of order and perception. Namjoshi, along with her contemporary feminists, believes that the modes of perception proffered to the reader are governed by the patriarchal dominance that needs to be critiqued. For this, Namjoshi invokes the familiar world of fairy and folk tales, gives them a feminist angle and re-presents them to convey new meanings to suggest an alternate social order. The emphasis in Namjoshi's works has been to break the tradition—both in theme and narrative strategies. Her identity as a lesbian feminist actuates her to contravene the boundaries imposed on women and her identity as a creative writer of the twentieth century presses her to invert novel strategies of presenting the same. Therefore, Namjoshi fuses the genres of fable, myth, fairy tale and folk tale to unmask the subjugation of women.

Namjoshi's impulse to look into the traditional tales from a different viewpoint reflects her life philosophy. From the very beginning, Namjoshi took decisions differently in order to be something in her own right. Born in a highly influential Chitpavan Brahmin family of Pune, Namjoshi had a position of authority right away. Her strong determination to prove herself led her to become an Indian Administrative Service Officer, the most highly regarded government position in India even today. Soon she left 'bored' with the power that it brought and took study leave to get a Master's degree in Public Administration at the University of Missouri, Columbia. The government job made her learn how to stay out of trouble, which bothered the author so much, that she resigned in 1969 and moved to Montreal, Canada to pursue her Ph.D. at McGill. Her subsequent thesis on Ezra Pound and lectures at Scarborough College, Toronto University, refined her creative sensibility to a great extent. A lesbian from India, a fact that she admits in *Goja: An Autobiographical Myth*, Namjoshi began to participate in Feminist and Gay Liberation movements and developed her political and ideological positions reflected in her later works:

> *You have to be sensible you know. In India these things cause a scandal. A little discretion would have made a world of difference. . . .* Do you think it required no courage to come out and say explicitly as so many people did: "Yes, I'm lesbian, or yes,

> I'm homosexual," and so gradually remove the disgrace from these words? (*Goja* 111)

In 1988, Namjoshi resigned from her teaching position to settle down finally with her lesbian friend and partner, Gillian Hanscombe, in Devon, England. Suniti Namjoshi explicitly expresses her rejection of the heteronormative structure in her works. In order to present alternative modes, she defies the normative in form and content by mixing various genres together. Heteronormativity as a norm is challenged with the construction and deconstruction of the 'populist gendered system,' as Helen Merrick puts it. On the one hand, Judith Butler considers gender as performative, not as a ritual but as a repetition, Helen Merrick endorses the view that the "slippery term 'gender' refers to the socially constructed attributes and 'performed' roles that are mapped on to biologically sexed bodies in historically and culturally specific ways" (*Ibid.* 240). Janice Raymond contends that one needs to differentiate between sex and gender. The sex of a person is unchangeable but the performance of gender varies from person to person. According to her, the material body remains the same and the object of study is the gendered social behaviours that we attach to them. Judith Butler adds that heterosexuality forces stereotyped gender roles to reinforce normative sexuality and the subordination of women. Identities whose performance is non-normative such as butch and femme identities or homosexuals or bisexuals account for the 'Gender Trouble' in society.

Suniti Namjoshi's characters range from the familiar fairy tale protagonists like Cinderella, the Red Riding Hood and Rapunzel to the classical ones including Miranda, Antigone and a female Caliban. C. Vijayasree comments: "through her poetic works Suniti Namjoshi illustrates a very different picture of female. In her poetry we find some times a very strong, firm and a woman with distinctive attitude. On the other hand, sometimes she is as tender, sensitive and transient as a petal of a flower. Her female characters like Miranda or Caliban are masterpiece creations. Her texts move beyond endings and eschew closures. Here it is relevant to quote Helene Cixous's point of view on feminine text that states, a feminine text, "is always endless, without ending: there's no closure, it does not stop." (Vijayasree 159)

Subverting the classical myth of Caliban, Miranda and Prospero in Shakespeare's *The Tempest*, Namjoshi in *The Bedside Book of Nightmares* lays bare the power politics of patriarchy. In an interview with Chelva Kanaganayakam, she admits that when she had read *The Tempest*, she felt sorry for Caliban because this creature was the king of the island. She considers Ferdinand, in comparison with him, a wimp and Prospero, a rude father. "Snapshots from Caliban" politicizes race, gender, class, nationality, language and hegemony by presenting a female Caliban who writes a journal and records her love, grief and suspicions in the form of a diary. Prospero, the father of both Caliban and Miranda, is a manipulative ghost who fails to understand that he has created them:

> I made them? Maiden and monster
> and then disdained them?
> Was there something in me
> that fed and sustained them?
> Are they mine or their own?
> I dare not claim them. (*Ibid.* 102)

Miranda, the unruly daughter, is at first jealous of Caliban but the two gradually become "sisters," a nightmare for the postcolonial imperialistic and patriarchal sage who fails to understand their reunion. In *Because of India*, Namjoshi establishes herself as a third world lesbian poet writing the poems to "explain the bloodier aspects of gay liberation" for which she creates a Caliban with a strong ego: "who just wanted what she wanted" (*Ibid.* 83). Harveen S. Mann clarifies further:

"Namjoshi, however, defies the practice of male, postcolonialist dialectical appropriations of Caliban-as-colonized-and-resistant-man by recasting Shakespeare's character as a Third World lesbian subject. Concomitantly, she re-imagines Miranda as a desirous and murderous homoerotic figure and Prospero as the excluded and, finally, defeated patriarch, thereby offering another intervention in both the continuing history of *The Tempest* as (post)colonial narrative and the evolving, conflicted history of global feminism. (100)

In "From Baby F with Much Love," Namjoshi creates a female Frankenstein, Baby F, the family structure from the female perspective. The Baby F strives and struggles to define the space of women in the family, she evinces how women are tutored to be passive and submissive. Baby F's ego is inflated and then subsided when she reconciles with her mother but is prevented from becoming another meek anonymous woman. Tanu Gupta and Rajni in their article titled "Women and Patriarchy: A Study of Suniti Namjoshi" elucidate that myth-making enables the writer to "evaluate her identity, perceptions reordering the world and value systems projected in the past." Further, the female Frankenstein or Baby F "becomes the epitome of her spirit, her lesbianism & her inner conscience. Suniti Namjoshi had coined the character Baby Frankenstein to reveal her feelings towards her mother. Frankenstein conceives a creature and creates it. However, the creature becomes ugly and has some kind of supernatural strength. The ugly creature is not included in the human society. He gets higher knowledge through books. He has all basic human needs and sentiments. Frankenstein tries to control the creature. But he is not tamed. Frankenstein gets killed by his own created creature. In turn, the creature of Namjoshi is the lesbian daughter. The myth reveals the crisis between a mother and a daughter. Probably in this poem Suniti Namjoshi has tried to convey inner resentment of her spoiled relationship with her mother and a daughter." Tanu Gupta and Rajni further point out that the first verse itself validates their stance:

> It might have been simpler, mother,
> if you had found me in a cabbage patch,
> green and round and exceeding healthy.
> Then you could have eaten me.
> Or if I had been a caterpillar
> and you had been a leaf. (From *The Bedside Book of Nightmares* 7)

In "The Reformed Antigone" the female protagonist is wise enough to save her own life and decides not to bury her brother while in "Archetypes" Penelope expresses her rage in her weaving. By revising the classical myths and the fusion of poetry with prose, Namjoshi uncovers the sexist implications in these classical tales.

For Namjoshi, "patriarchy is 'fiendish' and, thus, in league with other Indian and Western feminists: "it is crucial that gender oppressions be exposed, debated, and redressed. Numbers of feminists located in the West, the Third World, and in interstitial spaces in between, have discussed across the 1990s and into the twenty-first century ways of brokering the rights of gender and sexuality while paying respect to the many other axes of difference that inform women's lives. Given the patronizing legacy of most forms of middle-class Western feminism, the cross-border dimensions of such discussions have often been difficult, and liable to self-destruct." Thus, she weaves fabulation and poetry in *The Blue Donkey Fables* that combines tigers, monkeys, rabbits, pigs, cats, magpies and other animals with a clever feminist blue donkey who tells stories and recites poetry in order to comment on human frailties and follies. The fables bring numerous animals together who unite to talk about issues ranging from the nature of art and poetry to the relation between appearance and reality. As to why the fable is chosen over other forms, Namjoshi offers an "Explanation" in the form of a short poem:

> Why do you write about plants and animals?
> Why not people?
> Because
> no daffodil shrieks to be plucked,
> no lily rages, 'admire my bower.'
> And if dogs go about and shit
> Their shit at least it mixes
> with the stones and mud . . .
> Someone explains,
> 'A tree is not a person. A boy is not a cat.'
> 'Yes,' I reply, striving for patience,
> 'that is the problem. Precisely that.' (*The Blue Donkey Fables* 6)

The predicament of immigrant women poets in a white male dominated society is illustrated in a sequence in which the blue donkey sets out to recite some of her verse to a lady in love with poetry. The lady's scathing comment of refusal to listen to the donkey expresses the marginalization of the non-white poets:

> 'I think poetry is so beautiful. I feel I could live on poetry and fresh air forever.' The Blue Donkey edged closer. 'Well, as it happens,' she ventured diffidently, 'I am a poet. Perhaps you would like to recite some of my verse?' 'Oh. Oh no,' the Lady replied hastily, then she recovered herself. 'The fact is,' she explained, 'that though I have studied many languages and my French and German are both excellent, I have never mastered Blue Donkese. And though I have no doubt whatsoever that your poems are excellent, I fear they would fall on untutored ears.' 'But please, I speak English.' The Blue Donkey could hear herself sounding plaintive. 'Oh,' murmured the Lady. 'But surely as a Blue Donkey, integrity requires that you paint the world as it appears to you. And consider: what have a lady and a donkey in common?' (*Ibid.* 25)

Suniti's confrontation of a feminine experience in an alien environment is satirically portrayed in the blueness of the donkey which positions it as different by virtue of species and colour combined with her claim of being a poet. K. Satchidanandan endorses that the diasporic experience is not just a question of voluntary or involuntary migration. One also needs to delve into the class and gender factor while cogitating on the writings of diasporic writers. If the first generation involuntary migrants faced racial and cultural struggles, the second generation including Gayatri Chakravorty Spivak and Amartya Sen went in search of better prospects, were 'resident aliens' and strived to politicize their identity. He extends his contention by saying that the immigrant experience of a refugee Bangladeshi or Philippine worker in Saudi Arabia or an academic capitalizing on his/ her scholarship in his/ her language or literature in an American University ought to be entirely disparate. The encounter of the aforementioned cannot be the same as that of a pagan Indian, Chinese or Mexican immigrant of the 19th century, or even worse, the African immigrant workers treated as "filthy, uncivilized slaves and beasts." Like class, language also plays a vital role as the experience of a writer writing in English from England, U.S.A., Canada or Australia, in terms of accommodation, negotiation and reception, is different from that of a writer writing in English in France or Gujarati in England. Further, "the diasporic experience is also a gendered experience, it comes to the writing of Indian women abroad, say Meena Alexander, Panna Naik, Malati Rao, Sudha Chandola, Sujata Bhatt, Anita Desai, Kamala Markandaya, Bharati Mukherjee, Suniti Namjoshi, Jhumpa Lahiri and others."

It is this gendered experience that makes Namjoshi portray in the Blue Donkey's insistence on remaining a blue donkey against a red bridge till she is accepted by the community serving as a protest in its own right. The stark blueness of the donkey projects the problematics of colour, race and sex in a white patriarchal construct. Suniti Namjoshi herself exclaims: "The interpretation of the fables in the West and here can be different too. In *The Blue Donkey Fables*, the donkey is discriminated against because its colour is blue. This was seen as a protest against racism in the West, while in India it was seen as a feminist protest. Here too a kind of racism exists in the form of the caste system and there are various kinds of snobbery. I meant it as someone bullying another." Chelva Kanaganayakam also finds Namjoshi "unable to participate in the conflict between centre and margin, between colonizer and colonized. In fact, one of her principal strategies is to avoid the creation of a character within a recognizable ethos, for to do so would be to recapitulate to the paradigms of patriarchy." (1996: 211) Therefore, Namjoshi combines fables in prose that are often poetic, with other poetic genres, particularly the sonnet, to castigate all—poets, feminists, literary critics, readers and patriarchs, as put forth by Diane McGifford. Her choice is articulated in her own words: "Of course, the fable is much closer to verse. It's much closer to poetry than the realist novel, and that is why I am pleased that I write these fables in what looks like prose or what is prose." (Qtd. *Configurations of Exile* 54)

Fantasy, fable and science fiction are also employed in *The Mothers of Maya Diip*, where Jyanvi, an Indian lesbian poet, enters an all-woman world and exposes the sexual preferences in patriarchy. The narrative alternates between the female dominated Maya Diip, the male dominated Ashagarh and the island of Paradise rid of permissible gender codes. Maya Diip is a matriarchal world working on the principles of love, unity and universal motherhood. With outsiders like Jyanvi the poet and Valerie, an American expatriate, Namjoshi critiques the hypocrisy of the heterosexual patriarchy responsible for the objectification of women. In its place, a separatist community of women or an alternative matriarchal utopia is posited as a desirable solution to women's subjugation. Hence, subversion and inversion of the traditional narratives becomes central to Namjoshi's works to deal with issues of gender and feminism. Uma Parameswaran readily supports Namjoshi's efforts: "But we cannot do without myths and metaphors. Indeed they are the basic tools with which a writer uses language as a creative process in a community which distances itself from that writer. Subversion is a powerful way of getting things across. Suniti Namjoshi does it marvellously in her retelling of the myths." (22)

Despite Suniti's denial of investigating the immigrant dilemma and the fact that references to India remain minimal in her writings, it is precisely this dislocation as an Indian that serves as the basis of her works in order to explore the polemics of belonging or, in actual, non-belonging. The homeland rooted in the mind are the 'suitcases' of a diasporic writer, as Vijay Mishra puts it, figures subtly in Suniti Namjoshi's writings. Born and brought up in Maharashtra, she admits that she depicts the landscape of Maharashtra in her books. Although she had not been educated in Marathi, the Marathi insight is grounded in her psyche and is consciously or unconsciously reflected in her works.

The fabulist mode of writing by picking birds, animals, witches, gods and goddesses has definite parallels with the Indian culture. Apart from the inversion of classical Greek and Roman archetypes of Philomel and Perseus, Namjoshi's fables are inhabited by monkeys, crocodiles, swans, foxes, fishes, lions and mice that are encountered in Indian conventional fables and folklore. Indian fabulist literature involves an element of wit that is mirrored in her fables when she makes a feminist point with humour and understatement. Her fables are also infused with harshness, irony, clarity and sensibility of the Maharashtrians. She acknowledges it thus: "If you get anything that is Indian in my writing, that is a Marathi sensibility; it is there in the sensibility, not in the content. Marathis are known for their sarcasm and for their irony. You cannot offer a compliment in Marathi without sounding as if you were being ironic or teasing." (*Configurations of Exile* 48)

Although Suniti's feminist ideas were shaped in the West, one can trace their roots in the Indian philosophy. In *Same-Sex Love in India: Readings from Literature and History*, Ruth Vanita argues that the Indian literature and Hindu mythology proffer abundant instances of homosexuality and transgression of gender. She debates that Buddhism and Hinduism provide some examples of the undoing of gender. In Buddhism, a lot of women become bodhisattas and finally attain Buddhahood. Buddhism asserts that no human is born with intrinsic 'masculine' or 'feminine' traits. 'Shunyata' or 'emptiness' is the only reality: "The goddess explains: just as you are not really a woman but appear to be female in form, all women also appear to be female in form but are not really women. Therefore, the Buddha said all are not really men or women. . . . All things neither exist nor do not exist. The Buddha said there is neither existence nor nonexistence." (Ruth and Kidwai 22)

Ruth Vanita also holds that apart from 'male' and 'female,' the concept of 'third sex' was also coined in Indian culture and was admitted into Sanskrit grammar in the sixth century B.C. The attainment of the third sex was the most intense desire that could be experienced by both the 'male' and 'female' sex. Further, friendship is given a remarkable place in Indian culture and heritage and apart from the categorization of women in relation to men as the virgin, the widow and the courtesan, there are women in love with friends with whom they played in their childhood or are similar to themselves.

Friendship forms the primary theme of the Indian text *Panchatantra* literally meaning five *tantras* or narratives, strategies or theories—a compendium of stories that travelled to Europe in the sixth and eighth centuries. *Panchatantra* depicts animals as protagonists that perform human actions or behaviour.

The stories present "odd" friendships between members of different species that deconstruct the notion of gender and sex. In Ruth Vanita's words: "At least one of these implications could relate to gender and sexuality. If the categories 'man' and 'woman' are socially constructed as both opposite and complementary to one another, playing out the action between beasts rather than humans could have the effect of defamiliarizing and undoing the categories." (*Ibid.* 41)

The most famous narrative is about the friendship between the monkey and the crocodile that sets as an example of love between the same sexes. The "odd" friendship becomes the key concern of the crocodile's wife who starts to consider the monkey as her foe and decides to destroy him. The wife fails to comprehend that the crocodile, which feeds on flesh, can be friends with a he-monkey. She accuses her husband of having clandestine relations with the monkey presuming it to be a female. The quotation from the *Panchatantra* denotes the ardent love between the two male friends: "If she is really not your beloved then why don't you kill her when I am asking you to do so? Again, if the creature is truly a male ape, as you say, what kind of affection is this that you fell for it?" (*Ibid.* 45)

Suniti Namjoshi's exploration of the motif of friendship and same-sex love surely reflects her Indian influence as she agrees to have read the *Panchatantra* in her interview with Chelva Kanaganayakam. The notion of lesbian intimacy and a woman's love for a fellow woman is not only based on her understanding of Western feminist theory, but also her reading of homosexuality depicted in Indian traditional fables. Whereas in the *Panchatantra* the crocodile's wife questions his queer affection for the he-monkey, Namjoshi's version of the fable, 'The Monkey and the Crocodiles' finds nothing strange in this association:

> A monkey used to live in a large jambu tree which grew along the banks of the river Yamuna. The fruit of this tree was unusually de-

> licious and a bit like plums. At the foot of the tree lived two crocodiles. The monkey and the crocodiles were very good friends. The monkey would feed the crocodiles plums and the crocodiles in return would make conversation. They also protected her—though she did not know it—by keeping a watchful eye on her. (*Feminist Fables* 29)

In tracing evidences of same-sex love in Indian texts, Ruth Vanita shows that homosexuality and the notion of fluidity of sex have been the core themes of the *Puranas*. The love story of the two Hindu gods, Shiva the destroyer and Vishnu the preserver, is a fine illustration. Shiva gets attracted to Vishnu and adapts the Mohini form in order to entice him. The sexual play of Shiva and Vishnu followed by Mohini's pregnancy results in the birth of Hariharaputra—which literal means the son of Vishnu and Shiva—symbolic of the union of the two opposing forces of destruction and preservation. The story also recounts that later Vishnu transforms into the Mohini form to obtain the ambrosia—the juice of immortality. Mohini is absorbed back into Vishnu and does not endure a separate existence thereafter. Further, Vanita elucidates that Hindu gods changed their sex in order to demolish demonic powers. She exemplifies this with the transformation of Krishna into a woman to destroy a monster. Other references point to the *Mahabharata* where Radha and her female friends (sakhi) play and bathe together and Krishna tries to invade their independent feminine space. Hence, the transcending of sex and gender in Suniti's works can be traced back to Hindu mythology. Her detachment from and active participation in the Indian culture is reflected in her poem "In That Particular Temple" where she celebrates lesbian love by invoking the legend of the dance of Shiva:

> When we make love
> you and I
> are both sacred and secular.

The goddess' limbs
begin to move.
Balanced underfoot
the world spins. (*Configurations* 45)

The Hindu view of the fluidity of gender and sex and the concept of arbitrary identity are best manifested in *The Conversations of Cow*. Namjoshi's personal profile as a lesbian herself residing with her partner explains her urgency to legitimize lesbianism in her writings. She is the first Indian woman to have declared that she is a lesbian who views heterosexuality as repressive social structure responsible for the subservience of women. As a lesbian she, therefore, wishes to define queer relations to the world. Namjoshi had been long questioning this in her works: "It's obvious that for some time now I had been asking the question, what was my place in a world that often seemed absurd to me? All right, I was a lesbian, a lesbian feminist. But who was a lesbian? What was her relation to other people?" (*Because of India* 83)

It is this dilemma of positioning a lesbian vis-à-vis the world that forms the subject matter of most of her works including *The Conversations of Cow*. Each culture uses certain specific animals to define the relation of self vis-à-vis the world. Uma Parameswaran asserts: "in her *The Conversations of Cow*, she [Namjoshi] superbly carries off three banners any one of which is enough to weigh down the average person: the banners that celebrate being a woman, a non-white woman, a lesbian and she does it armed with the two indispensables of a writer's toolbox—rage and humour." (22)

For the Indian culture, the cow is perhaps the best-known symbol today to denote the quest for self-identity. In "Embracing the Past by Retelling the Stories," Ruth Vanita once again points out that the cow functions effectively as a symbol for crossing boundaries of gender, nationality and sexuality:

> Nonhuman animals, being less containable than humans in categories of gender and nationality, often function, both in Eastern and Western mythologies and literary traditions, to undo these categories and to reveal the surprising commonality of apparently distinct traditions and groupings. Furthermore, the apparently uncrossable gulf between human and nonhuman may function as metaphor for the equally uncrossable, although socially created, sexual gulf between members of the same gender. (143-44)

Ruth Vanita delineates that the cow represents the woman-as-goddess-and-slave syndrome as well as the image of Mother India as an undernourished, overmilked, mindless producer of numberless children. On the one hand, the cow enjoys a sacrosanct status, an object of worship, addressed as 'Gau Mata' and Hindus are forbidden to eat the revered animal and, on the other hand, the cow is exploited by equating it to the female body. Vanita further adds that the cow has been attributed with several connotations in the English and Hindi language. For instance, "stupid cow" is an insult in English, indicating the female body as good for nothing except for procreation. When a woman is addressed as "cowlike" in Hindi the emphasis is on her innocence and patience. Therefore, Indians perceive the cow and woman interchanging their roles as objects of victimization. Subsequently, the cow becomes a symbol of the notion of the fluidity of identity in Hinduism.

The Conversations of Cow addresses the possibility of transformation of identity with the two main protagonists: the lesbian cow Bhadravati and the author Suniti. Bhadravati, the lesbian Brahmini cow, nicknamed Baddy by Western cows, which find it difficult to pronounce her name, is reminiscent of the author's own location in a foreign land: "'I ought to tell you,' Cow informs me, 'that this is a Self-Sustaining Community of Lesbian Cows.' I scrutinize Cow. So, Cow and I have something in common." (17-18)

Cow lives with her lesbian friends Bouddica, Cowslip, Lou-Ann, Ariadne, Sybilla and others. Bhadravati combines Eastern with Western literary traditions in her image of a Hindu goddess as well as a lesbian diasporic animal. In her transgression of sex, the Cow recalls the Hindu mythological cow 'Surabhi' who produces an endless stream of milk and 'Kamadhenu' or the wish-fulfilling cow. 'Dhenu' means 'cow' and 'Kama' means both 'wish' and 'work' and also 'erotic desire' and 'sex' as in *Kamasutra*. When all the wishes are fulfilled and no desire is left, one reaches the stage of 'Moksha' or liberation. Ruth Vanita upholds that Namjoshi's Kamadhenu helps to liberate her from her prejudices and categories.

During the course of her narrative, Bhadravati changes into an Indian woman who later becomes Suniti's lover. The lesbian cow-turned-woman then metamorphoses into a well-meaning white man named Bud, crossing the boundaries of nationality, race, gender and sexuality and so wishes to marry Suniti. The world, as explained by Cow, is forked into Class A and Class B humans:

> Class A people don't wear lipstick, Class B people do. Class A people spread themselves out. Class B people apologize for so much occupying space. Class A people stand like blocks. Class B people look unbalanced. Class A people never smile. Class B people smile placatingly twice in a minute and seldom require provocation. (24)

Cows contend that they can easily pass as men since both cows and men spread themselves out, stand like blocks without apologizing for occupying space and never smile without provocation. On the other hand, Suniti does not understand what she would like to change into and so tries to be a Class B heterosexual companion to Bud or Baddy, Bhadravati's white male persona. Cow's reference to her sister Charlotte, a six-foot-two blonde woman, despite being a Hindu and threatening Suniti of turning into carnivorous terrifies Suniti. The Cow is not troubled by her frequent transformations and tells Suniti: "'It's all right,' she says, 'identity is fluid. Haven't you heard of transmigration? And you call yourself a good Brahmin?'" (32)

Cow expresses her desire of being an ordinary animal and Suniti asserts her wish of being extraordinary, 'a mysterious stranger' (66). Suniti decides to remain cheerful in her status of a devoted wife of Bud but her life becomes miserable as an ordinary woman. However, she feels exhausted with this cheerfulness soon in coping with an unsatisfactory man and prefers solitude. Her sense of alienation and self-absorption is manifested in her waking up the next morning with her double Suniti 2 or 'S2.' Both Suniti and her chaotic split self 'S2' are wearied with the multiple identities of Cow and see the world reduced to nothing. Finally they accept Cow in all her selves as Western and Indian, as human and nonhuman, as man and woman, as heterosexual and lesbian:

> O Cow of a thousand faces and a thousand names, O Julia, Peter, Madelaine and Kate, O Margaret, Charlotte, Amy and S1, O Bouddica, Sybilla, Cowslip and S2, O Ariadne, Lou-Ann and Madame X, O Cow who manifests herself in a thousand shapes and a thousand wishes. (121-22)

The novel concludes with Suniti's double merging back into her and the acceptance of Cow in all her forms. Suniti decides to write the conversations in the form of a book and: "Cow as world becomes Cow as book. This is the last and also, in a sense, the first metamorphosis, the Word that is the end and the beginning of every conversation and conjuration" (Ruth 161). Makarand Paranjape sums it up thus:

> Gender, sexual preference, race, nationality—all these become freefloating signifiers eventually. Throughout, the protagonist must undergo the painful process of confronting herself in shifting relation-ships. Who am I? is thus the central query of the novel, a que-

> ry as old and profound as the Upanishads. In the end "Cow" learns that she is not determined by those markers that society uses to designate and manipulate identity; she can be anything she chooses to be. In the process of this realization there are touching and telling satires on several controlling metaphors of Western society, the idea of labelling a certain type of woman "Cow" being only one of them. This is a story of learning and growing into greater self-acceptance and wisdom. In the process the protagonist becomes more tolerant and more accommodating of others as well.

Suniti Namjoshi's confirmation of her lesbian experience is articulated further in *Goja: An Autobiographical Myth*, a heroic step in the confession of being a lesbian who crosses national boundaries to find a place for herself. Namjoshi recounts her childhood and adolescence in India with her aaya, Goja and grandmother, The Ranisaheb. Amidst the Maharashtrian landscape, Suniti relates her love relation with these two women, to whom she justifies her choice of remaining a homosexual amid the heterosexual patriarchal society. The writer narrates her lesbian experiences with three women, 'Paramour' a wood nymph, Christine and Gill. Paramour becomes the poet's inspiration with whom she falls in love in the 'enchanted forest.' Namjoshi is enticed by the woods, the leaves and the ambience and expresses her passionate love for her:

> I'm at home in this forest. . . . Paramour, of course, lives in the forest. She is the forest. Under enchantment anything is possible. Identity is lost, and with it fear. I'm a fawn in this forest. I put my head in her lap. The leaves and sunlight brush her nakedness—as I would, as I do. She feels my head against her thigh. She feels my tongue brush her hair. I embrace each tree trunk, each leafy branch to its very tip. For a while the forest and I float on darkness. (*Goja* 95)

Namjoshi's alliance with Christine helped her define her political and ideological status as a non-white lesbian woman who should advocate the rights of lesbians in a white man's world. Poetry, fables and prose fiction followed hoping for the recognition of lesbian needs and desires. The collaboration with Gillian Hanscombe subsequently declared Namjoshi's lesbian identity by moving to England with her and thereafter composing pure lesbian literature in *Flesh and Paper*.

The powerful outburst advocating alternate female identity could be seen as early as in "Various Reasons," published in her collection *Poems*:

> A policeman? He raised his hand? So.
> He said, "Stop." But is that poetry?
> Is that life? Now there are no policemen
> in my mind, neither traffic, nor otherwise,
> Tho' of course it's natural to assume,
> but stone walls do not a prison make,
> and by upbringing and birth I'm not a citizen
> of a police state. Not that I hate policemen
> and they don't really remind me of anything;
> But the policeman said, "Stop."
> And, my dear, they do exist.

Thus, Suniti Namjoshi delves deep into the question of female subjugation in a heteronormative world by reworking traditional myths and fables. Her pursuit of inquiry into the female condition and its portrayal with playful irony, wit and humour is a product of her Indian influence mingled with her feminist ideas shaped in the West with the readings of Adrienne Rich and other radical feminists. Alternative spaces need to be sought as the writer violates national boundaries or gendered boundaries or even nations seen as gendered constructs by theorist-critics like Benedict Anderson, Gayatri Spivak, Michel Foucault, and Partha Chatterjee who have demonstrated that "modern nationalism is a gendered construct that favours male hegemony and idealizes the woman-as-mother (country)-of-nationalist-sons." (Mann 106)

Suniti Namjoshi's immigrant status may not have provoked her much to describe the racial, cultural and social inequities faced in an alien environment, yet it is the very fact of being an Indian that has promoted her to write for the cause of women. Her declaration of being a lesbian and the will to overthrow the patriarchal dominance has formed the very basis of her works and given shape to her fantastical conception of a lesbian separatist commune fully articulated in *The Mothers of Maya Diip*. The Indian law and the society have expressed their resistance to homosexuality which instigates the writer to venture into alternatives outside patriarchy that, in turn, urge her finally to "have a political need to sustain and celebrate the woman-woman bond as between subject and another subject, rather than conceding anything to the subject/ object model typical of heterosexual patriarchy—spelt out for us by Simone de Beauvoir, so long ago." (Qtd. York 157)

Feminist Fables and *The Mothers of Maya Diip*: A Critique

> Do not start. Do not blush. Let us admit in the privacy of our own society that these things sometimes happen. Sometimes women do like women. (Virginia Woolf, 1929)

This chapter proposes to apply Suniti Namjoshi's theory of lesbian-feminism as elucidated in the previous chapter to critically analyze *Feminist Fables* and *The Mothers of Maya Diip* that deal with women's oppression and posit separatism as a positive solution to patriarchal suppression of women. A similar and earlier idea was postulated in the poem "We Can Compose Ourselves" from the collection *Because of India* where the two lesbian partners Suniti Namjoshi and Gillian Hanscombe propose to 'invent' a country where lesbians can stay separately: "We can compose an ocean if we like. . . . Or we can compose ourselves. But a politics? To invent, just we two, a view? How to think? What to do? And a country? . . . In yours [your country, India] . . . though even the rocks have names, we wither, having no word. And in mine [England] the word is so raw it bleeds; and from fury of pain, it attacks; and would maim us daily." (122)

C. Vijayasree defines a lesbian as "the rage of all women condensed to the point of explosion. She is the woman who, often beginning at an extremely early age, acts in accordance with her inner compulsion to be a more complete and freer human being than her society—perhaps then, but certainly later—cares to allow her. These needs and actions, over a period of years, bring her into painful conflict with people, situations, and the accepted ways of thinking, feeling and behaving until she is in a state of continual war with everything around her and usually with herself." (72)

Feminist Fables was first published in 1981 at a time when Canadian feminism had already arrived at a mature stage in this development. It was the dawn of lesbian feminism with organizations such as LOOT and National Lesbian Forum fighting for the rights of lesbians in society. Namjoshi had been visiting Sappho and the Gateways and meeting lesbians and gay men. Her lesbian friend Christine Donald had influenced her most with her feminist ideas. It was some of the remarks that Namjoshi made that jerked her to write something for the cause. It went like this: "Here in the West, all that seems to matter for social status is gender and money. But in India several factors operate: caste, class and family background. An Indian woman who has all these factors operating for her certainly isn't oppressed. And it seems to me that such women are far less awkward and far more assured than many of the women I've seen here." (*Because of India* 78)

Soon, Namjoshi realized that her remark was utterly stupid and that she had been ignoring and disregarding women for whom these factors operated. It was this realization that produced *Feminist Fables* during her sabbatical leave in 1979. Namjoshi's *Feminist Fables* is a result of the Canadian feminist and lesbian-feminist ideals interwoven with her Indian heritage. It is the mingling of her Indianness with her lesbian perspective that forms the structure of her fables. She concedes that the journey to deviate sexually was not so easy for her. Suniti discusses her mother's strong opposition to her sexual orientation in an interview with Christine Cryoden: "She has never been particularly happy about that I'm a writer, or, a lesbian feminist. She sees these as notoriety, tarnishing the good name of the family." (Gupta 121).

If fables are designed to solve human problems, Namjoshi's use of fables is idiosyncratic. Etymologically, a fable is derived from the Latin word *fabula* which means a made-up story that carries the suggestion that a fable has nothing to do with truth. Yet, traditional fables are seen as potential carriers of "truths," of patterns of behaviour of a particular culture. If fables and myths have been used for serving pedagogical needs, Namjoshi "uses this essentially moralizing and instructive genre in a satiric way," and "sets herself against the 'truths' of a given order." (Dasgupta 103) Unlike traditional fables, where generalizations are applied to individuals, her fables address idiosyncratic individuals engaged in particular idiosyncrasies. So, her fables reveal a truth ratified by her conscious lesbian feminist identity and her insights into the nature of "truths" structured in conventional tales.

A fable is linked to the proverb that claims to be a universal repository of truths. Hence, it becomes crucial that fables depict types and not individuals. But Namjoshi's fables break the very notion of cultural stereotypes of the masculine and the feminine. Her three-fold marginalization of being a lesbian woman writer of the Indian Diaspora is manifested in the fables where she develops the 'Asian perspective,' the 'alien perspective' and the 'lesbian perspective.' (*Because of India* 22) The fables are set apart from the conformist to express the concealed "truths"—the underlying patriarchal hegemonic codes embedded in them. In *Because of India* she reports, that for her, the fables "were a way of exploring feminist ideas and their implications for the patterns I had inherited through the mainstream literary tradition." (79)

The two fundamental elements of a fable are the presence of non-human characters engaged in human performance and the moral of the story. Thus, we have the non-humans teaching the humans lessons of life. As far as this is concerned, Namjoshi's fables also contain birds and beasts tutoring their human counterparts. Yet, the fables are distinctive as these characters do not enact the conventional role of preaching the moral or ethical discourse. Namjoshi's characters range from animals such as ducks, swans, lizards, monkeys, crocodiles, mares, snakes, mongooses, bears, ostriches, foxes and owls to mythical characters like Red Riding Hood, Little Miss Muffet, Jack of the Beanstalk, Goldilocks and the Ugly Duckling and further to the invented ones such as the handsome young dyke, the New Woman and the Incredible Woman. In an interview with Chelva Kanaganayakam, she says: "I am always asked why I write fables and why I write about animals. I try to supply answers, but the honest truth is I don't know. We don't separate animals from human beings. As for animals talking, why not?" (Kanaganayakam 1995: 50)

Unlike traditional fables, most of her characters are females registering their protest against the system. Her fables have a feminist rendition and reworking enabling her to trace and reveal what is unsaid and undermined in the patriarchal structure rooted in them. In her essay "When We Dead Awaken: Writing as Revision" Adrienne Rich observes the significance of reworking traditional narratives from a gynocentric perspective: "Re-vision—the act of looking back, of seeing with fresh eyes, of entering an old text from a new critical direction is for us more than a chapter in cultural history; it is an act of survival . . . this drive to self-knowledge, for women, is more than a search for identity: it is part of our refusal of the self-destructiveness of male-dominated society." (1993: 167)

Feminist Fables offers a new vision into the condition of women in society in a male governed world. Through inventing a new mythology, they question the oppression of women in patriarchy and suggest alternatives. With playful irony they investigate the position and fate of women in heterosexuality. In her article on *Feminist Fables*, Savita Goel comments: "In these hilarious, witty and elegantly written fables, she [Namjoshi] has invented a mythology that is simultaneously thought-provoking and entertaining and deals with the aspects of women's lives that have been erased, ignored, demeaned and mystified." (177)

What are the issues raised in these fables? How does Suniti Namjoshi bring to the fore the ill treatment faced by women? If one looks at the fables closely, one may find them as an explication of the three phases denominated by Elaine Showalter—the 'Feminine,' the 'Feminist' and the 'Female.' The fables explore the 'feminine' aspects in women when they are accustomed to succumbing to the wishes of men and comply with the dominant modes of behaviour dictated to them; the 'feminist' phase where they protest against the values and demand autonomy; the 'female' phase where they summon women to search for their identity. The fables highlight the fact that gender inequity is not a biological but a social construct. Gender differences are constructed consciously for empowerment of women and Namjoshi's fables deconstruct these differences and identities as well. Sabine Steinisch remarks: "Namjoshi leaves an open space which is there for her readers to fill. It is exhilarating to watch her characters insistently resist fitting into conventional patterns, but at times one's smile freezes in the face of the biting sarcasm with which Namjoshi points to the intolerance these patterns have generated. Her stories circle around the problem of finding a subject position as a woman in relation to men, to other women and to society in general." (Steinisch 271)

Retelling of old myths and tales has been a dominant motif in the Canadian feminist tradition. Upending traditional tales and the conformist gender roles in order to accentuate feminist ideas has been witnessed in the writing of contemporary Canadian feminist writers and Namjoshi seems to be in league with her contemporaries. From the rewriting of old popular ones like 'The Ugly Duckling' and 'Hansel and Gretel' to the invention of new ones like 'The Doll' and 'Owl'—the ontology remains the same—the unmasking of the subjugation of women from heteronormativity.

Ramya D. classifies the hundred feminist fables employing Anderson's *Tales of Panchatantra*, Aesop's Fables, Greek myths and other Christian myths into three broad categories—the first containing fables about traditional and modern women, the second set retelling the classical myths and the third and final set advocating her lesbian feminist ideology. C. Vijayasree says: "The issues raised in these fables are of course basic to the human condition: Intimacy, loneliness, death, anger, ambition and desire, and these thread their way through their collection and are explored now with an eye for the comic, for the absurd, now with a sense of poignant sadness and longing." (76)

The first fable 'From the Panchatantra' is the story of a Brahmin who prays to Lord Vishnu for a son but instead gets a daughter. Still, he imparts all his knowledge to her to make her a Brahmin. After much meditation Lord Vishnu reappears and the Brahmin again asks for a son. In his next birth, the Brahmin becomes a woman and bears eight sons. Namjoshi ends the tale on a satiric note that sums up the entire collection. This time the girl asks for a human status and the god sneaks away with the words, "Ah, that is much harder." (*Feminist Fables* 2) With skillful irony, the author reveals that women have been denied human status and human rights.

In 'The Little Prince' the conventional order of men ruling and women obeying is reinstated. The fable is about an ambitious queen who fortunately desires that her daughter should ascend the throne. So, she deliberately brings up the little prince as demure and shy and the princess as adept in all skills—hunting, tennis, mathematics and law. Somehow, she convinces the king that the more capable should rule and so the tests for various skills are set. The prince fails and yet the idea of being ruled by a woman infuriates the king. Order is restored as the prince ascends the throne and the 'wicked queen' and her 'unlucky daughter' are banished forever.

Often Namjoshi's fables are pithy and concise and end on a crisp note that implies what she wishes to convey. 'The Tale of Two Brothers' is a perfect citation which needs to be quoted fully to validate the above: "There was once a man who thought he could do anything, even be a woman. So he acquired a baby, changed his diapers and fed the damn thing three times a night. He did all the housework, was deferential to men, and got worn out. But he had a brother, Jack Cleverfellow, who hired a wife, and got it all done." (36)

The fable is a tongue-in-cheek satire on the servile status of women performing household chores, taking care of the children and being obeisant to men. In 'The Secret Wisdom' the servility is again articulated when a young woman in search of wisdom visits the Country of Smilers. In an interview with its leader, she interrogates the secret of their wisdom. The leader explains to her that the countrymen utilize their energy economically by listening to and looking at unpleasant things with the left ear and eye respectively. He further adds that the natives are trained in this art. When the woman servant serves the refreshments and the young woman inquires if she could learn how to make them, he replies that she requires no training for it, as being a woman she is suited to it: "'My dear,' said the leader, 'don't worry about it. You have a natural talent for our native discipline. You need no training.' She was extremely pleased and smiled brilliantly." (41)

Usually fables contain animals wearing the human garb and enacting their conduct. Namjoshi's fables also have numerous animals and beasts stating feminist ideas and morals. In a scoffing tale 'No Frog in Her Right Mind' the fabulist pictures the immurement of women in a patriarchal set-up. The fable is about a prince who catches a female frog while playing and takes it home. At home, he puts her in a jar and all night long the frog struggles to escape. Her efforts succeed and she flees at dawn. The prince gets up in the morning and, not finding the frog in her place, goes outside carrying the jar. The title suggests that the frog's attempt to defy the norms and move out of her defined space are futile as the prince would trap her again. Women have grappled hard to transcend the domestic space in quest of freedom and men have fettered them by displaying their manhood over them.

What is the fate of women who remain restricted in the space allotted to them? Namjoshi hints that if women remain subservient without complaining and submit to the wishes of men, their existence is bound to fade into oblivion with their identity extinct. She allegorizes this in her fable 'The Derbyshire Fish.' The Derbyshire Fish represent those women who have never tried at moving outside their homes and surrender to the patriarchal norms willingly. In the narrative, the writer tells that the fish found in Derbyshire in the English Midlands are blind as they swim in the dark. They are also transparent as they do not see and prefer not to be seen. It is only when a child notices some dead fish in one of their caverns that their existence is acknowledged. The fish, according to the story, are dying because they do not want to breathe in fresh air and sunlight: "But the fish keep dying. The conclusion is inescapable: nature knows best, these benighted creatures do not wish to live. It will all work out. They are nearly extinct." (85)

The height of this subordination is brought out in 'Her Mother's Daughter' in which there is a couple who has a feminist daughter. As the daughter grows up, she decides to avenge the wrongs done to her mother. The mother is shocked as subservience is rooted in her psyche and the idea of going against the said norms is almost irritation for her. The daughter tries hard to explain to her mother how patriarchy has made them dependent on the father and that they should fight for their liberation. The horrified mother makes it clear to the daughter: "in a good patriarchy the women are dependent, but they're not allowed to know it," and "that's how it should be." (96)

Namjoshi's fables allege that daughters are trained from childhood itself to be passive, patient, and complaisant and to "hold their tongues." The first instance of this is shown in the fable 'The Lesson' where a young girl, after having been inspired by the naked emperor of the noted fairy tale 'The Emperor's Clothes,' undresses herself and believes herself to be an emperor. Her mother, at once, chides her and passes on the right lesson: "Don't be silly darling. Only little boys grow up to be Emperors. As for little girls, they marry Emperors; and they learn to hold their tongues, particularly on the subject of the Emperor's clothes." (8)

The silencing of women is also divulged in 'Nymph' which is the reworking of the myth of the Greek god Apollo chasing Daphne and the latter being transformed into a laurel. The fabulist gives us three cases where the nymph turns into a laurel. In the first case, the fabulist picks up the traditional myth and questions if silencing is the fate of women who are unwilling to succumb. In the second, she twists the tale by saying that the nymph is willing and chases the god instead. The god soon gets bored and the nymph is again turned into a laurel, as she needs to be muzzled. In the third case, Daphne yields and keeps quiet afterwards. She is changed into a green laurel: "it obviously means, that trees keep quiet." (4) In an interesting fable, the author observes that the birth of a girl child is not taken to be a cause of jubilation till date. 'The Local History' is the tale of a young girl who is also a goddess of a small fishing village. In one particular year, there is shortage of fish and a stupid young man persuades the villagers and uses her as bait to have fish in bounty all the time. The fishers try to amputate and drown her but the goddess does not die. They are disappointed and gradually their lives change. They forget fishing and the goddess but remember one thing. They celebrate the birth of a son with joy and the birth of a daughter with grief.

Patriarchy makes women extremely vulnerable to objectification and commodification owing to their acquiescence. Namjoshi unveils this aspect of patriarchal autonomy as well in her fables. In one of the fables 'The Milk-White Mare' set in the times of the Caliph, Prince Haroun-al-Rashid, "defender of the mighty and the protector of the loyal" (27), witnesses a woman transformed into a mare by magic being treated brutally by her husband and father. Earlier, the woman had been discarded by her husband believing her to be a slut. Having been transformed into a mare she was handsome and useful and was desired by both the men. The Prince does justice: he gives each of them fifty gold pieces and the mare is kept in the stables of the Prince, thereby utilizing her utmost. The insinuation is also carried further in 'Legend' which projects how women have been objects of male gaze and commodified. The argument is advanced when a she-monster, found by a group of scientists, is operated, dissected and cut up; its bones scraped and kept in the National Museum, lest she causes any damage to the world if left unleashed. With undercutting irony, the fabulist ends the narrative by saying that the legend goes like this: "'The Dreaded She-Monster. The fumes of this creature are noxious to men.' Inscribed underneath are the names of the scientists who gave their lives to find this out." (33)

However, in 'The Dower,' Namjoshi suggests that the struggle of women against this commodification is required. The fable provides three different endings to the main plot. A king desires to have a son but has three daughters in succession. When the first one is born, the queen convinces him that wherever she will walk flowers will sprout. The second is so gifted that wherever she will walk pearls will be found. Unfortunately when the third one is born the queen dies and the girl is not considered to be a princess since her gait produces nothing. One day the princess' foot is cut and a ruby is formed out of her blood. Three probable destinies are possible according to the writer: the princess is not allowed to walk with shoes and the king turns richer by the day; the king marries her to a poor swineherd before the miracle occurs. Once her foot is cut and the miracle takes place, the couple sells the jewel to get the princess a new pair of shoes; the first princess becomes a florist, the second sets a pearl business while the third produces a ruby when it suits her.

Heterosexual patriarchal hegemony that reduces women to objects of sexual gratification is yet another theme of *Feminist Fables*. Namjoshi skillfully plays upon language to show how women unknowingly relinquish and consider it their duty to satisfy men's sexual and emotional needs. 'Scheherazade' is one of the feminist fables where the writer plays upon this notion. Men engage themselves in gazing at women and women, in turn, make themselves apt objects of male gaze. If women fail to please their sexual counterparts, women are made to pay the price in patriarchy. The fable juxtaposes horses with humans and the male sex of both the species overpowers the female sex: "Watch how the stallion mounts the mare. Watch how the mare submits to the stallion. So the Caliph at night will mount the princess. The princes will give much pleasure to him. This is the law. It pleases Allah." (45)

Once the Caliph is bored with the princess, she will die. The stallion has one thousand mares and the Caliph has one thousand women respectively for their pleasure. In this manner, women have been victimized serving men and satisfying their needs. In another myth of the 'Green Slave Women,' the idea is further confirmed as the Green Slave Woman, irresistible to men, is tamed and forced to surrender to the Space Captain by exercising his physical prowess on her. "His sexual swordplay, his inexhaustible energy, his amazing acrobatics" result in the final submission of the woman. (67)

The worst damage done to women in patriarchy is their loss of individuality and reduction to being subservient attendants to their fathers and husbands. Before marriage they must preserve their chastity and after marriage apply their coquettish skills to appease men. Virginity is a jewel to be safeguarded till marriage and later worn and enjoyed by the husband. 'Jewel' shows a young toad who is worried about losing the jewel on her forehead after marriage. The parents console her that when married, she will be the sole property of her husband, who will be the sole owner of the jewel and then, "it really won't matter whether or not you are precious." (55) The taboo of chastity is yet again critiqued in a brief fable about two knights and a damsel in 'Complaint.' A damsel in distress is raped by one of the knights who abduct her. The other knight—the lover—combats with him and wins. Ironically, it is not the girl's complaint about her wretched state but the knight's complaint that he cannot marry her since she has lost her virginity. Maidenhood or purity is also the central theme of 'Blood' where the feminist fabulist explicitly talks about the concept of bleeding associated with the first act of sexual intercourse. In the fable the Snow Maiden is pure and white and her "breasts white and virginal." (35) The prince marries her believing her to be a virgin. When he makes love to her, the Maiden does not bleed. The prince is provoked and abandons the Maiden.

The clichés associated with women are 'stupid,' 'weak,' 'fragile,' 'insipid,' 'demure,' 'imperfect' and 'inferior' to men. In contrast men are 'rational,' 'brave,' 'strong,' 'bold,' 'flawless,' and, undoubtedly 'superior' of the human species. Wisdom, knowledge and strength are manly qualities alone. *Feminist Fables* also reveals the binaries as proposed by Helene Cixous.

The French feminist analyzed that, in mainly all binary oppositions, activity/ passivity, father/ mother, head/ emotions, intelligible/ sensitive, the underlying opposition is man/ woman and woman has been perceived as secondary, passive and powerless. In her utopian vision, women will get rid of this logocentric ideology that silences women and will become creative in a non-oppressive and non-sexist society. She also opposed the term *écriture feminine* or 'feminine writing' as terms like 'feminine' and 'masculine' are rooted in sexual difference. For her, the work holds more significance than the sex of the author. 'The Gods' is a fable about an old couple gifted with a girl child who is precocious and surpasses everyone in running, music and studies. She is truly blessed by the gods with great abilities, yet the men of the village are judgmental: "to be so damned good, is not womanly." (37) This is again corroborated in 'Whore, Bitch, Slut, Sow' in which a strong-minded woman pleads to the Judge that the labels that she bears must be changed. The judge tries hard by calling her a thief or a beggar or even a bastard but the scholars argue that she is neither of these: "'The truth is, your honour,' the scholar replied, 'that her wickedness consists in the fact that she is a woman.' 'Ah,' said the Learned Judge, 'That is the answer. Go away, Woman, that is your name and your new label.'" (26)

Similarly, in 'Myth' Namjoshi shows that women have been considered accountable for the damage caused to human civilization since its creation. The narrative is about the constant wars between the demons and gods, the former having a winning edge, as they are granted the milk of a goddess which has recuperative powers. The gods understand this and implore the goddess to give them her milk too. Motherly and beneficent by nature suited to a woman, the goddess yields and the wars, thus, rage forever. "Whose fault is it? It's her fault, she gave in" (101).

Having revealed the cultural archetypes of the masculine and feminine, Suniti Namjoshi next offers a stage of protest, the 'feminist' state against this oppression. Through her fables she arouses women to rise out of their slumber and get ready to rebel against patriarchy. The 'Bird Woman' projects this freedom in women where the parents of a she-bird, whose wings begin to grow at a rapid speed, refuse to cut them in order to teach her to fly. The action signifies the liberation being gifted to the bird to fly wherever she wishes. In 'Liberation' she transforms herself into a colourless bird to experience independence. The concept of liberty in Namjoshi's fables is elucidated by Savita Goel: "Liberty for her means the deconstruction of social structures, so that they do not retain the shape which men have given them and she is fully aware that the world belongs not only to men but also to women." (181)

The retelling of 'Perseus and Andromeda' is also designed to play upon cross-dressing and the subversion of gender roles. The original fable shows how the prince fights with the dragon each time to save the princess in danger. In Namjoshi's fable the princess has a mind of her own, and when tied to the stake, she lures the dragon into changing their roles. The dragon becomes the prince, the princess becomes the dragon and the prince is tied to the stake. The prince is left alone while the dragon and the princess leave. Namjoshi implies that women who acquire an independent identity can do away with gender constructs laid down by the society. 'Rescued' is the refashioning of Rapunzel's thoughts when she is trapped in the witch's castle. Rapunzel, in Namjoshi's fable, dreams of the prince coming to rescue her. Displeased with the dream, she dreams of liberation in the truest sense: "She dreams of a castle with a very wide moat and four strong walls and a room of her own where she is perfectly safe." (87)

The next fable 'Jack's Three's Luck' reworks the traditional 'Jack and the Beanstalk' to undermine gender boundaries and to incite women into freedom from cultural constructs. 'Jack's Three's Luck' has Jack with his two brothers who climb to the top of the beanstalk and confront a giantess. The giantess agrees to marry them if they are willing to obey her and perform the household chores. Jack and one more brother disagree but the third one relents. The giantess marries him immediately and loves him and is kind to him and the writer concludes: "it's entirely possible that they lived happily ever after." (98)

'Swayamvara' promotes the choice of partner for women. The fable recounts a princess adept at whistling and so sets up a whistling contest for her suitors. She beats each one of them and asks if they consider themselves beaten. All the suitors but one considers it unmanly to acknowledge his defeat. The princess marries the one who does and the Swayamvara is over. 'The Doll' deals with the overpowering of the female over the male sex. Two little girls make a male doll and name it 'Brittle Boy.' A boy comes along, gets infuriated, and breaks it. The girls are also annoyed and "would like very much to smash the boy. But they say to themselves that the boy is fragile. They pick up the sticks, and start over." (103)

The feminist rendition of the fairy tales 'Cinderella' and 'Hansel and Gretel' contribute to the ideological protest of the fabulist. 'And Then What Happened?' tells us that after marrying the Prince, Cinderella realizes that the marriage has not been a fair bargain. The Prince accuses her of having married her for his money and the latter blames of having done so for her looks. Their marriage is not a just decision and Cinderella walks out. The fairy tale heroine flouts all conventions and bravely decides to end an unhappy marriage. The other tale 'In the Forest' violates gender codes once again. This time Gretel is the stronger of the two and encounters the witch whereas Hansel hides behind a tree. Gretel lives with the witch while Hansel goes back to his stepmother, for "when he grows up to be a man, he will fight them all." (93)

Feminist Fables also depicts women undergoing the process of self-discovery. After having cognized that they have been victims of repression in more than one way, women have come a long way in their struggle for emancipation. They have comprehended that their ultimate source of solace and freedom resides outside the shackles of patriarchy. A lesbian herself, Namjoshi feels that lesbians must be recognized in society with their due right to exist freely. Therefore she endorses the idea of women living with women outside the fetters of patriarchal set-up. She is conscious of the indignity attributed to a lesbian which is brought out as well in these fables. The utopian vision of a woman-identified world is most explicitly apparent in 'The Moon Shone On.' The fable describes the love of two women unable to find words to express their love for each other:

> 'I love you,' she said in despair to her friend. 'And I you,' said her friend . . . soon they were entwined in one another's arms. And then? And then the moon shone on, the grass was green, flowers sprouted, it was probably spring, they were lovers after all. (49)

Suniti Namjoshi celebrates lesbian identity and consciousness in 'The Badge-Wearing Dyke and her Two Maiden Aunts.' Two spinster mice live together and are visited by a niece. The niece wears a number of badges such as 'Gay Liberation is our Liberation' and 'Lesbians Ignite.' The niece explicates that she wears these badges to protest against the discrimination women suffer when they love one another. The two mice comfortably tell their niece that they have been living together for the past twenty five years. They argue that "on the whole, one is so much comfortable with one's own sex" (11) and the niece takes off her badges and gives these to them. According to Oliver Ross, in this short fable, "explicit signifiers of homosexuality such as 'gay' and 'lesbian' are juxtaposed with an ambiguous relationship between two women which oscillates between homosocial companionship and same-sex eroticism. There is no clear moral regarding the validity of these expressions and embodiments of love and sex; instead the fable troubles ideas of sexuality, a vociferous LGBT politics, and the subsumption of diverse practices and identities of female-female desire into a grand narrative of lesbianism. Political movements such as that embraced by the lesbian protagonist must avoid the flattening of difference, the fable implies, if they are to be ethically viable." Lesbian feminists see women free from the emotional dependence on men which is demonstrated in Namjoshi's fable 'For Adrienne Rich—if she would like it.' The tale is about Scheherazade again who, after a thousand and one nights, is given the offer of becoming the Caliph's queen as a reward. After a thousand and one nights of dying repeatedly, the female protagonist chooses to free herself from the bondage of heterosexuality and chooses to live with her sister Dinarzade as a reward.

Namjoshi's critique of heterosexuality is also evident in 'The Wicked Witch' where a young dyke visits a witch to solve her dilemma. The dyke falls in love with a woman who refuses to accept her, as what she feels for her, is not the Real Thing. The Real Thing is the love between opposite sexes which is considered normative in patriarchy. The witch advises the dyke to convince her that what she feels for her is equally real or get a large group of people to persuade her that her same sex love is the Real Thing. The woman tells the witch that she cannot do so and the witch then asks her to find what she really feels by starting right then in the witch's home.

Despite this promising vision of an exclusive space for women outside the coercive forces of patriarchy, Namjoshi is mindful of the criticism and abuse lesbians have to face. The fate of lesbians in a heterosexual reality is sad and depressing which forms the motif of the next fable 'A Moral Tale.' The narrative states the moral that homosexuality is disapproved in society and, thus, the fate of homosexuals is surely a tragic one. In the traditional fable, the Beast is in love with Beauty. The author turns the conventional narrative upside down by making the Beast a woman who is in love with another woman. The Beast is unconventionally gentle and non-belligerent. The girl does not accept the Beast's love that, in turn, becomes desolate: "She becomes more and more solitary and turned to books. But the books made it clear that men loved women, and women loved men, and men rode off and had all sorts of adventures and women stayed at home." (23)

'The Example' sets an example of the hurt suffered by the lesbians in society. Two sparrows hire a wren as a tutor for their children but soon they discover that the wren is a lesbian. The wren reasons that her sexual choice has nothing to do with her teaching but the parents get worried lest she might corrupt the children morally. They call her 'dreadful' and 'horrid' to which she protests: "'I am not dreadful and I am not horrid,' said the wren indignantly. 'That makes it worse. You set an example,' said the parents sternly. 'So do you,' said the wren." (56)

Lesbians not only do not enjoy the basic rights in society but are also denied human status. 'Troglodyte' deals with a woman cave-dweller who falls in love with another cave-woman. She is unable to understand her emotions: "it may not have been love, perhaps it was love, or perhaps friendship." (68) She draws large number of sketches of the other woman and expresses her love. In time, both of them die and fade into oblivion: "By now it is firmly established that this woman never was, that she never painted, and never lived." (68)

Thus, *Feminist Fables* exposes the exploitation of women on social, sexual and psychological grounds. The fables divulge the inadvertent submission of women in patriarchal dominance and revitalize women to break the bonds that deny them the freedom they deserve. As a lesbian feminist, Suniti Namjoshi commemorates the love of women for women within the restraining heterosexuality. Diane McGifford asserts: "though her fables teach and have animals as teachers, her lessons usurp the status quo to endorse feminine thought . . . and coax the reader to the inevitable conclusion that women have been silenced and men have not." (293)

> 'I would make everybody behave themselves,' Alice said firmly.
> 'How?'
> 'Well,' began Alice. (Suniti Namjoshi, 1991)

If *Feminist Fables* promotes same-sex love, *The Mother of Maya Diip* envisages a lesbian feminist utopia establishing the writer's lesbian identity forthrightly. *The Mothers of Maya Diip* is a prose fiction that mixes myth, fable, the novel, satire, science fiction and fantasy to propose an all-women world and also reminds of *Gulliver's Travels.* The conceptualization of creating a world where women are privileged over men, where good will and sisterhood prevail, where men are totally absent is derived out of the need to realize social structures free of heterosexual patriarchal hegemony. According to Charlotte Bunch, the lesbian is in perpetual revolt against the rich, white and male-dominated society:

> In our society, which defines all people and institutions for the benefit of the rich, white male, the lesbian is in revolt. In revolt because she defines herself in terms of women and rejects the male definitions of how she should feel, act, look and live. To be a lesbian is to love oneself, woman in a culture that denigrates and despises women. The lesbian rejects male sexual or political domination; she defies his world, his social organization, his ideology, and his definition of her as inferior. Lesbianism puts women first while the society declares the male supreme. Lesbianism threatens male supremacy at its core. When politically conscious and organized, it

> is central to destroying our sexist, racist, capitalist, imperialist system. (83)

Before one ventures into the fantastical projection of Suniti Namjoshi's matriarchal utopia, one needs to deliberate on the conceptualization and history of 'utopia.' The discourse can be initiated with the difference proposed between utopia and the utopian impulse by Philip E. Wegner where he elucidates that the latter is a strong urge to have an utterly transformed, other than real existence, exhibited in various works of literature and even Hollywood films like *The Godfather*. Wegner endorses Darko Suvin's definition of utopia where a quasi-human society more perfect than that of the author is created, consisting of harmonious individual and socio-political conditions. (Suvin 36) Quasi-human stresses that the world posited is to be discriminated from mythology or other forms of literature based on divine or mystic or fantastical characters. The utopian genre focuses on the larger collective socio-cultural machinery rather than individuals or individual characterization. Further, the utopian text is based not on a hypothetically ideal but a 'more perfect' principle—highlighting the negatives or failures of the existing social order and envisioning change—for the betterment of the Homo sapiens.

The term had come into being in 1516 in Thomas More's *Utopia.* Also, such ideal societies had been represented even earlier in Plato's *Republic* and *Laws* or in the works of the classical authors Pindar and Hesiod. Following Thomas More, one witnesses a proliferation of literary utopias with Francis Bacon's *The New Atlantis*, James Harrington's *The Commonwealth of Oceana* and Tommaso Campenella's *City of the Sun*. The eighteenth century saw significant developments in this field with Jonathan Swift's *Gulliver's Travels* and the French writer Sebestian Mercier's *The Year 2440: A Dream if There Ever Was One*. Whereas the former is, what Sargent would call, a "Utopian satire," the story of Lemuel Gulliver and his four sea journeys criticizing not only the English middle class but humanity at large, the latter accounts the tale of a contemporary of Mercier who dozes off and wakes up to find himself in twenty-fifth century Paris that has changed dramatically.

The theorist Lyman Tower Sargent defines utopia as "a non-existent society described in considerable detail and located in time and space" (Wegner 80) accentuating the fictional status of the utopian society as well as its location in imaginary time and space. Sargent goes on to demarcate varied categories—the "eutopian or positive Utopian," where the author gives us a non-existent society better than the society in which the reader lived. In contrast to this, there is the "dystopia or negative Utopian" where the author intends us to see a society considerably worse than that of the reader. On the one hand, in "Utopian satire" the vision offered is "a criticism of the contemporary society" and on the other hand, "anti-Utopian" serves as a "criticism of Utopianism" which Sargent also terms as "social dreaming." The last category in this typology is the "critical Utopian," where the society envisaged is "better than contemporary society but with difficult problems that the described society may or may not be able to solve, and which takes a critical view of the Utopian genre." (*Ibid.* 81) Further, Raymond Williams classifies four types of utopias: "(a) *the paradise*, in which a happier life is described as simply existing elsewhere; (b) *the externally altered world*, in which a new kind of life has been made possible by an unlooked-for natural event; (c) *the willed transformation*, in which a new kind of life has been achieved by human effort, (d) *the technological transformation*, in which a new kind of life has been made possible by a technical discovery." (203)

The categories, however, overlap and the negative of each can be further distinguished as the classification of dystopia.

Conversely, we get "(a) *the hell*, in which a more wretched kind of life is described by existing elsewhere; (b) *the externally altered world*, in which a new but less happy kind of life has been brought about by an unlooked-for or uncontrollable natural event; (c) *the willed transformation*, in which a new but less happy kind of life has been brought about by social degeneration, by the emergence or re-emergence of harmful kinds of social order; (d) *the technological transformation*, in which the conditions of life have been worsened by technical development." (*Ibid.* 204)

On the one hand, Jean Pfaelzer and R.M.P emphasize that the dystopian world is a world of entropy and decadence, albeit justify the need of an egalitarian society; on the other hand, Ernst Bloch has faith in utopian visions of the future. He endorses the view that if humanity is too entangled in the present then there will be no imagination of the future. Subsequently, Wegner catalogues various Utopias ranging from William Dean Howell's *A Traveller in Altruria* to Arthur Dudley Vinton's dystopia *Looking Further Backward* to a woman's utopia in *Herland* by Charlotte Perkins Gilman. The most noted utopias written were Orwell's *Nineteen Eighty Four* and Aldous Huxley's *Brave New World*. The Second World War saw the flourishing of dystopia with Philip K. Dick's *Martian Time-Slip*, Harry Harrison's *Make Room! Make Room!* and the most famous being Margaret Atwood's *The Handmaid's Tale*. Anti-Utopians and Dystopians announced the emergence of true feminist Utopian traditions in the 1960s with Ursula Le Guin's *The Dispossessed*, Joanna Russ' *The Female Man*, Ernest Callenbach's *Ecotopia* and Marge Piercy's *Woman on the Edge of Time*. The 1980s resulted in a new hybrid, known as the "critical dystopia." These works "look quizzically, skeptically, critically not only at the present society but also at the means needed to transform it." (Wegner 92) The 1990s witnessed the publication of works that posit other worlds with newer and better resources. Alasdair Gray's *A History Maker* is set in a future Scotland and Nalo Hopkinson's *Midnight Robber* draws upon Caribbean traditions in a new imaginary world.

Utopian fiction had gained prominence during the Renaissance and the nineteenth century. As the fate of the social revolution was sealed at the beginning of the twentieth century, writers of utopia soon got disillusioned with its 'totalitarian' approach and shifted their focus to dystopic visions. The traditional utopographer presented a fixed stable locus borne out of his/ her imagination. The utopia was presented to the audience with the aim of enforcing the writer's ideology. Such an authoritarian structure needed to be amended which happened only at the end of the twentieth century where the utopias expanded their horizons with open-endedness. As Bulent Somay and R.M.P. elucidate: "The utopian writer who cannot (or does not want to) take an authoritative stance has to do away with the "present" paradigm of the traditional utopian text, thus opening up the utopian horizon while calling for the imaginative co-operation of his or her audience. A *doctrinaire*, or *dogmatic*, utopian text does not substantially deviate from the traditional utopia, which asserts the utopian locus as "ultimate" and drastically limits the possibilities of the utopian horizon; an *open-ended* text, on the other hand, portrays a utopian locus as a mere phase in the infinite unfolding of the utopian horizon, thereby abolishing the limits imposed on it by classical utopian fiction." (26)

With the emergence of Thomas More's *Utopia* in 1516, the concept of the perfect society came into being where the obstacles of the real world were done away with. The earlier concept of the traveller, a 'He' not a 'She' would tour to a far-off land where the state of affairs would obviously be perfect and the reader would locate the anomalies of his own world directly or vicariously. Greed, theft, hunger, jealousy and all other vices would be removed and peace and harmony would be restored. Yet, critics in the twentieth century have objected to such utopias as dystopic, as the state becomes all domineering and the individual will is suppressed and crushed in such idealistic visualizations.

How far, is then, a Utopia, an objectively ideal society? This question has been deliberated, at length, by critics and theorists. If Thomas More was a Catholic, his utopian vision was monastic. What followed was a wave of writers whose views oscillated between capitalism and socialism as the perfect solutions for utopias depending on their times and the writer's ideology. Wegner concludes that utopians have always responded and will always respond to sweeping historical changes in the world. Utopias have primarily hypothetically equated human with man. The feminine gender was either excluded or completely subverted: "Women have tended to play supporting roles as the 'others' of men—emoting bodies to their reasoning minds and nature to their culture. Only rarely women have been represented as subjects in their own right." (*Ibid.* 126)

According to Joanna Russ: "Utopias are not embodiments of universal human values, but are reactive; that is, they supply in fiction what their authors believe society . . . and/ or women, lack in the here-and-now. The positive values stressed in the stories can reveal to us what, in the authors' eyes, is wrong with our own society." (*Ibid.* 129) With the feminist movement gaining momentum in the 1960s, women writers like Ursula Le Guin, Marge Piercy and Pamela Sargent, thus, expressed their concerns for the oppressed gender in their utopian blueprints. Arthur C. Clarke goes to the extent of presenting a utopia and then letting it fall to point out its flaws in his *Childhood's End.*

The gender divisions and prejudices have been questioned and refuted by women who have conceived matriarchal visions, antithetical to the conventional models of utopias, where women gain potential to perform the role of the superior sex and men have been perceived as the 'alien other.' The "battle of the sexes," to borrow Joanna Russ' term, does not end here. The successfully scientific matriarchies are also mocked at by texts like Francis Stevens' *Friend Island* or *Via the Hewitt Ray* by Margaret F. Rupert. Gender role reversals have also been seen where women perform masculine duties such as Susan Calvin is the leading female scientist in Asimov's Robot series, the intellectual female characters in Heinlein's *Tunnel in the Sky* and *Have Spacesuit will Travel*.

Tatiana Teslenko defines feminist utopianism as a certain trajectory that has the potential for community building and political reformation. She endorses that the traditional utopias do not envision gender equality and fail to bring out the sexual iniquities within the hegemonic patriarchal system. The feminist utopian texts expose this sexist approach and woman's subordinate position in patriarchy. Angela Warfield adds: "Feminist utopian discourse is ostensibly an ideal form of this expression and has the ability to turn traditional—what Teslenko calls patriarchal—utopias on their heads and offer us a new way of seeing the world. These novels go beyond mere thought experiments to have real-world effects on social structure and inspire political action. Feminist utopianism also rides the wave of postmodernism's subversion of grand narratives and "welcomes the opportunity to rewrite the patriarchal script." (Warfield 324)

Teslenko supplements the discourse with the view that feminist utopias offer openness and multiplicity by circumventing dogged social constructs, what Lucy Sargisson coins as 'Transgressive Utopianism' in *Contemporary Feminist Utopianism*, which is an expression of "multiplicity rather than an all-encompassing perfection." (*Ibid*. 325)

Suniti Namjoshi's lesbian feminist agenda reaches its zenith with the propositioned matriarchal utopian state Mayanagar in

The Mothers of Maya Diip casting women as the positive dominant sex and the men as negative, as the 'other' in relation to women. Since men are perceived as subordinate, women can deconstruct and reconstruct masculine and feminine codes. Inversely, masculinity symbolizes beauty and meekness and so the boys are addressed as 'pretty boys' just as women have been customarily reduced to petty objects worthy of male gaze.

The Mothers of Maya Diip, the lesbian utopian fiction, begins with a vision of matriarchy that "bloomed ashamedly" (113) in one of the princely states of India that is considered to be a forbidden land for the inhabitants of a patriarchal society. Shyamala A. Narayan finds *The Mothers of Maya Diip* an unusual novel of fabulistic fiction and "Maya Diip is an Indian principality visited by Jyanvi and the Blue Donkey (who appeared in *The Blue Donkey Fables*, 1988). Here they find a rigid matriarchy, which has escaped many of the evils of male-dominated conventional society; but it is plagued by other problems born of common human failings like jealousy and love of power." The Ranisaheb or the Queen of Mayanagar invites the Blue Donkey along with her friend Jyanvi to the Maya Diip. The Blue Donkey has pledged celibacy and Jyanvi is a poet and a lesbian—reminiscent of the author's identity. The pun on the title brings out the paradox—'Diip' meaning a lamp and 'Dwip' meaning an island. 'Maya,' on the other hand, signifies 'compassionate' or 'illusory.' Therefore, Maya Diip can be best understood as a sort of refuge for women, enlightening them in their quest of self-identification, a compassionate matriarchal hypothetical world which is both compassionate yet illusory.

The Matriarchy is headed by the Queen or the Ranisaheb, the Matriarch of the Mayan Council, the other members of the Council being the Five Lesser Matriarchs of the Five Great Families. The Council is, however, answerable to the Chief of the Guilds. The Guilds are the various groups that are allotted specific functions—the Guild of Poets, the Guild of Goddess' servants, the Guild of Mathematicians and so on and so forth. The hierarchy of mothers is maintained with three-tier structure of mothers—Grade A, B and C. The Grade C are the lowest grade mothers and function as workers performing the task of rearing the daughters borne by the Grade A and B mothers. The Grade C mothers toil religiously; pass several tests of proficiency before applying for Grade A status. The Grade B mothers are simply biological mothers. The Grade A mothers are those who have qualified as perfect mothers and are expected to have daughters right away. Although they are the epitome of motherhood, yet they do not take care of the daughters directly. They may bear their own daughters or allocate this job to the Grade B mothers. The Grade A mothers barring the Matriarch eventually become the Chief of the Guilds with all the other mothers as members. The Guild of Poets is led by Pramila the Poet; the Guild of Therapists is headed by Shyamila the Civil; the Guild of Goddess' Servants by Shyamila's lover Sarla Devi. The Ranisaheb or the Matriarch is portrayed thus: "She was a Grade A mother three times over (that was the maximum), she herself was the product of a Grade A mother three times over, she had an excellent appetite, she was always clad in green, and she always prevailed, or, at least, she frequently did." (117)

The Queen is regarded as the incarnation of the Supreme Mother and matriarchy is, thus, passed on to successive generations: "in practice the bloodline has been unbroken for seven hundred years." (127) The Matriarch has four biological daughters—Asha, Shyamila, Pramila and Saraswati. Pramila, Shyamila and Saraswati are the rightful heirs to the throne that leads to corruption in Mayanagar subsequently. Maya Diip maintains an army in the form of the Guild of Therapists in place of the police steered by Shyamila the Civil in order to deal with crimes, not of violence or of aggression, but of "maladjusted mothers, unsisterly sisters, rivalries and jealousies of diverse sorts, non-conformity with Mayan customs, and, of course . . . the problems of lovers." (128) Although the Matriarch is the Supreme Mother, the citizens of Maya Diip worship the Goddess who prophesies the future of the Mayans on the auspicious 'Day of Oracles.' The temple of the goddess is maintained by the Guild of Goddess' Servants under the guidance of Sarla Devi. The Guild of Therapists and the Guild of Goddess' Servants are the two most powerful guilds in the Mayan society.

At the core of this blissful utopian matriarchal world is the commemoration of motherhood. The Mayans uphold that motherhood makes the life of a woman complete and purposeful. Unless a woman becomes a mother she is not granted adulthood. So, young girls are coached to become good mothers. Gagri, the Good, the Matriarch's granddaughter undergoes several tests of her skill with babies to qualify as a good mother before she is permitted to go out and play. Hatred for children or negligence of duty of raising the children is sacrilege in Mayanagar. Shyamila the Civil narrates the story of a girl who wished to spend time with the pretty boys and refused to behave like a womanly woman devoid of maternal feelings. The young girl was abandoned by everyone and implored on the streets frantically to become a mother. The story focuses that the matriarchal utopia has no place for women who do not consider motherhood imperative to their existence. The mothers of Maya Diip earn their livelihood by taking care of the children in the best manner possible. Power becomes significant for the employment of lesser grade mothers as subordinates. The Grade A mothers hire the Grade C mothers in the same fashion as men engage their 'wives' to fulfill the household duties. The more powerful the mother, the more favoured the child and to take care of the more privileged daughter becomes a privilege for the Grade C mother.

Every love relation on Maya Diip is a relation of co-mothership. Lesbians hoping to wed and live together must opt for raising a common daughter, for they are "not just two women who can live by [them]selves," but are "members of a society with a part to perform." (147-48) Performance, in turn, is directly related to the financial gains in the form of multiple bonuses. The finances are distributed according to rank which is allotted according to birth as well as merit by the Coffers of the Guilds, the Five Great Families and the Matriarch. The illusory Mayaland, like any other state, glorifies motherhood and idolizes children as long as they are female. The concept of father is foreign to the Mayans which is exemplified when Jyanvi reports, that in her society, she had applied for the status of co-mother but was denied on the grounds that a father would be more useful to which the Mayans express their curiosity in knowing what a father is! Further, to question the sanctity of the state is heresy and the consequential punishment of heretics is banishment. For this reason, Asha is exiled from Maya Diip who contested that male children deserve a better status.

Within this Strirajya, there are outsiders who expose the hypocrisy of the system. An American expatriate Valerie's account of the socio-cultural milieu in a heterosexual patriarchy caustically communicates the fact that Maya Diip is nothing short of a patriarchy turned upside down where women rule a world populated by women only. Women are located at the centre and the men at the periphery who are considered to be useless creatures with no identity of their own. Male children addressed as 'pretty boys' are milked for their semen and then forsaken under the 'Tree of Death.' Those who manage to survive commit suicide in their teens. Apart from this, men have no role to play in this absolute women-identified set-up of "no individual isolated and each woman bound to the others by ties of kinship, accepted loyalties and professional affiliations." (128)

Unlike in a patriarchy where women are relegated to a subordinate status, Mayanagar has the Rule of the Mothers, which is "gentle" and "generous." But, like a patriarchy, it suppresses one sex to exalt the other. Even violence and aggression, which are withdrawn completely from the society, by the elimination of the males, "survives as a well-hidden secret in the forms of atomic weapons stockpiled on the island." (Dasgupta 108) Whereas in a patriarchy, both the sexes are raised and nursed together and "the pretty boys grow to a larger size and attempt to rule" (137), in Mayanagar, the male children are deemed mad at their age of puberty, when they begin to fight among themselves, and then the waves, and eventually turn into foam. In a heteronormative society women fade into oblivion; in this matriarchy men are waste except for their semen for reproduction. However, Valerie's satiric portrayal of her homeland where men enslave women and make war on them to have babies—a land of male masters and female slaves—makes Maya Diip a definitely better alternative to reside in and explains why she has no intention of repatriation.

J. Elizabeth Clark and Katie Hogan affirm: "feminist writers, such as Charlotte Perkins Gilman in *Herland*, Marge Piercy in *Woman on the Edge of Time*, and Suniti Namjoshi in *The Mothers of Maya Diip*, have sought to present readers with Utopian visions of societies created by and for women. This work [*The Mothers of Maya Diip*], primarily labelled science fiction because of the disjunction between everyday life and the fantasy (or a sometimes dystopic critique), seems impossible to bridge." The narrative, therefore, begins with the Blue Donkey and Jyanvi entering Mayanagar and the latter falling in love with Saraswati who is a Grade A mother with a daughter named Sona. Namjoshi mingles poetry and prose as Jyanvi recites poetry in order to express her love for Saraswati: "arms, legs and limbs/ the curve of your throat/ when the goddess made you" (115).

Since a love relationship in Maya Diip is primarily one of co-mothership, Saraswati interrogates whether Jyanvi would agree to take this responsibility. Jyanvi, on the other hand, has no inclination of bringing up children and is only interested in marrying Saraswati. In a poetry recitation function, while the other mothers celebrate motherhood through their poetry, Jyanvi arrives at an opposing point of view. She expresses her indifference towards children by positing them as obstacles to love:

> They were clean, and quick and sprightly,
> They scampered in the sun.
> 'I must go,' I said politely,
> and left true love alone. (132)

Despite Jyanvi's dislike for children, she is appointed as a Grade C mother for the welfare of Gagri the Good, the Matriarch's granddaughter and heir and the daughter of Asha the Apostate, who has been exiled for her blasphemy. The Day of the Oracles arrives and the goddess forecasts that the one who suffers change and yet remains the same will become the next Matriarch. It is assumed that Saraswati shall reign successively and so corruption in Maya Diip sprouts first seeds.

Part II of the narrative takes us to an alternative place, Ashagadh that is an all-male utopia headed by a woman, the Matriarch's daughter, Asha the Apostate. The prophesy results in the expatriation of the Matriarch, Saraswati, Jyanvi and the Blue Donkey to the forest and Sona and Gagri the Good as hostages by Shyamila the Civil who usurps the throne with the help of Sarla Devi. Through their action, Namjoshi suggests that power is innately corruptive and the lesbian utopia falls short of turning into a dystopia. The Matriarch and others find shelter at Ashagadh or the Fortress of Hope which is populated by the young men rejected by the Mayans and stolen from the 'Tree of Life' known as 'Tree of Death' in Maya Diip and trained to become 'perfect mothers.' The young men also pass tests to attain adult status and beseech the 'Tree of Life' to grant them baby boys. In order to express their need for babies they carve short and wooden rods that represent the Tree itself.

The male utopia is on the verge of perturbation when Valerie acts as the Serpent in the Garden of Eden and corrupts the innocent creatures. Valerie explains the working of a heterosexual patriarchy to the young Ashans: "the Ashans enslaved the Mayans and divided them up among themselves. The more important the Ashan, the more he owned . . . only the Ashans mattered to the Ashans and only the Mayans mattered to the Mayans . . . that the Ashans had all the power. . . . Every Ashan thought of himself as a kind of farmer, and of every Mayan as a bit of land or a field which could be his property." (192)

Valerie elucidates that an Ashan is always a Grade A mother whereas a Mayan is always a Grade B mother. She acquaints the young Ashans with the concepts of slavery, rape and war that become a time bomb for the Mayans and results in the imprisonment of Valerie. Saraswati thinks that the Ashans are futile as they are warlike and sterile and cannot even reproduce but feels the need of these very Ashans to regain the Matriarchate of Maya. In return, Asha expects a change in the Mayan system with decent education and training for the young boys to make them capable Grade A and C mothers since they cannot become biological mothers. The Matriarch turns down the plea and the issue is left unsolved.

The crisis is resolved in Part III when a group of commandos, who turn out to be androids later, come to rescue Valerie despite her wish to stay. The androids seize her and the other women in their helicopter in order to take them to Paradise. Paradise, in this world, turns out to be an island inhabited by 'gallants' and 'mothers.' The gallants worship the mothers to the point of romantic adoration which makes motherhood a responsibility that no one is willing to take. The adulation of the gallants reaches its greatest heights when, having a shortage of mothers, they begin to kill themselves and start reciting some romantic poetry before dying: "When the Gallants commit suicide, they leave behind a couplet, sometimes a quatrain . . . it has become a custom, a tradition—the poetic thing to do—to die with a song on your lips." (229)

This extreme laudation and idealism turn out to be the rescuing aid for the mothers of Maya Diip. The Queen of Paradise and the Matriarch conspire to march on Maya Diip with an army of gallants to restore the lost matriarchy. The Blue Donkey is given the charge of the food supplies and the medical wing is appointed Supplier General and the Chief of the Medicinal Corps. Jyanvi, who shirks all responsibility, is commissioned the Commander-in-Chief of the Allied Forces of Air, Fire and Water. The gallants' eccentric behaviour gives them an opportunity to serve the mothers and the Matriarch's astuteness makes Shyamila the Civil and Sarla Devi capitulate and so the administrative powers are restored to the Matriarch. The abdicating Matriarch appoints Shyamila the Civil as the Supreme mother of the gallants accompanied by her lover Sarla Devi. Asha returns to her dominion and the Matriarch ends the narrative with the dethronement of Jyanvi—the woman who is least ready to take the responsibility as the successive Matriarch.

The Mothers of Maya Diip weaves fable and travelogues, utopia and science fiction, poetry and prose together in order to present a separatist community. From Mayanagar, the Mayans are transported to Ashagadh and then to Paradise in a helicopter. The gallants of Paradise club together as the Avians, the Fire Throwers and the Water Workers plot to produce a tidal wave to inundate the whole island. Just as both utopia and science fiction postulate a wishful construct of an historical alternative dealing with communities outside space and time of the author with satire implicit in them, Namjoshi's utopian science fictional text is located in a different space and time to propose a 'more perfect' principle and better organized communal relations. Anannya Dasgupta critiques: "both utopia and dystopia are conceptually related to the real through allegorical associations and represent possibilities to be accepted or avoided. However, in rejecting the idea of a separatist community, Namjoshi moves toward the "non-conceptual," a movement described by Rosemary Jackson as the opening up of "a space without/ outside the cultural order." (108)

In an article on Suniti Namjoshi published in *The Sunday Guardian*, Aishwarya Subramanian comments:

> If it both emulates and distances itself from feminist utopian science fiction, *The Mothers of Maya Diip* is willing to invoke (and discard) other genres as well. There's something of the epic about this story, with its arcane religious ceremonies, its power struggles between priestesses and queens. We are offered not one, but two fictional, fantastic city states. At one point the Ranisaheb and her entourage are cast out of the city and exiled to a forest. There's a bizarre science fictional interlude featuring a group of androids and a maternal helicopter. There's even a love story, most of the time about two people who are completely incapable of understanding one another. At the centre of it all is the Blue Donkey, sometimes treated as human and sometimes not, and devastatingly commonsensical in the face of all that is going on around her. It's her cool detachment from the book that allows it to be as odd a thing as it is, that makes thought experiments of its genres as well as of its fictional cities.

The moral of the fabulous fantasy is clear: the problem of women's oppression is grave and calls women forth towards radical reforms. Suniti Namjoshi's utopian fiction is surely a lesbian text written by a lesbian promoting lesbianism. She also explores "the different facets of lesbian desire and identity" within the framework of postcolonial discourse" (Rath 143). *The Mothers of Maya Diip* legitimizes that a woman's love for another woman is quite natural and that heteronormativity is a cultural construct. A woman's individuality is not only defined in terms of her relation to the male world but also in terms of her bonding with other women emotionally and politically. Lesbian writers also encourage the view that lesbians are not just two women in a sexual relationship but also those women who share quality time with one another. In the words of Lillian Faderman: "'Lesbian' describes a relationship in which two women's strongest emotions and affections are directed towards each other—sexual contact may be a part of the relationship to a greater or lesser degree, or it may be entirely absent. By preference the two women spend most of their time together and share most aspects of their lives with each other." (17-18)

The Mothers of Maya Diip pictures such a lesbian world where women are allied to each other in emotional, political and professional ties. Maya Diip conforms to the 'utopian' model characteristic of cultural feminism and radical feminism of the 1970s where women cease to co-operate with men on a daily basis, as explained by Sonya Andermahr, and see separatism as a final solution to the problem of women's oppression: "[We see] . . . lesbian separatism as . . . a viable, permanent alternative, which will prepare us for the time when we will be able to reinstate new forms of old matriarchal societies and when, once again, the Female Principle will have jurisdiction over the earth." (Qtd. AnderMahr 135)

The 'utopian' model of lesbian feminism emphasizes that a woman's identification with other women is total and exclusive. Women engage in a relationship of universal sisterhood in a quest of self-realization in and through the lesbian notion governed by the principles of solidarity and love. The model is a wish-fulfilment fantasy of sisterhood and mutual love. It articulates that emotional and psychological needs of lesbians have not been recognized in heterosexual patriarchy, and that, the said needs can only be fulfilled outside the purview of patriarchy. Maya Diip conforms to the norms of a utopia where women come together to overturn male supremacy. Women's needs and identities are preserved in a world devoid of men and celebrate the ideology of exclusivity. Samuel Gerald Collins writes: "women have felt the urgency to liberate women from these dominant clichés and thereby establish women as 'female super-heroes.' (Qtd. Collins 68) Jean Pfaelzer and R.M.P add: "If men have written their utopias or dystopias, they have depicted the perpetuation of female power as a threat to the family, biological and social life. Thus, they have resorted to stereotypes of women as "passive-aggressive, intuitive-logical, possessive-self-sacrificing, materialistic-spiritual, frigid-lustful." (68)

The Mothers of Maya Diip expands Adrienne Rich's notion of "lesbian continuum" as embracing "many more forms of primary intensity between and among women, including the sharing of a rich inner life, the bonding against male tyranny, the giving and receiving of practical and political support." (Rich 1980: 648-49) The text also validates that it belongs to the genre of lesbian literature as it paints strong images of women in love with each other, for instance, Jyanvi and Saraswati and Shyamila the Civil and Sarla Devi.

Through *Feminist Fables* and *The Mothers of Maya Diip* Suniti Namjoshi firmly supports that heterosexuality is not a preference but an imposition. Therefore, women are free to question it and present an alternative: "a freeing-up of thinking, the exploring of new paths, the shattering of another great silence, new clarity in personal relationships" (*Ibid.* 177). Although the utopia falls short of turning into a dystopian nightmare, Namjoshi maintains that it is definitely a more preferable choice to heterosexual patriarchal hegemony. Hence, the crisis is finally resolved at the end. Diane McGifford points out that Namjoshi understands that "power corrupts all and that even women must square their ideals with reality" (296). Yet, it is a better place to live in, a place: "no Mayan would want to escape" (146) and Suniti Namjoshi unites community with individuality, Western feminism and Eastern community to suggest that "community good and individual needs are the beginnings of a better society." (McGifford 296)

Akshaya K. Rath underlines the fact: "accepted notions regarding subject, sexes, personal spaces and narrative were thus violated in literature to bring in the writer [Suniti Namjoshi] and the reader a sense of transformation, relief, education and atonement and self-realization. Thus, Namjoshi's work recategorizes the connections between ethnicity and sexuality. Personal facts about lesbianism and bitter enactment of a racial self in the Western world provide Namjoshi a quest to develop such perspectives. These facts do not however come without a fortified ground of subjugation. The counter site constructed in Namjoshi remains operative in other collection of poems as well. Everywhere it is with a purpose—often political that Namjoshi creates the alternative space for the representation of women and for their liberation from the hegemonic world order." (Rath 153) To conclude, Suniti Namjoshi has carved a niche of her own in postcolonial queer discourse by provoking the reader to look beyond a world which is primarily heteronormative and malecentric. Alternate sexualities, subversion of the defined structures of gender, class and nationality, postcolonial discursive space of defiance of the said and the formation of the unsaid, thus, form the fundamentals of her literary corpus. In addition, Suniti's non-compliance of the canonical and the generic in favour of the fusion of myths, folk narratives and other tales in poetry and prose mark her unequivocal contribution to postcolonial women studies.

Bibliography

Adamson, Nancy, Linsa Briskin and Margaret McPhail. *Feminist Organizing for Change: The Contemporary Women's Movement in Canada.* Toronto: Oxford, 1988.

Anderson, Hans Christian and The Brothers Grimm. *The Best Fairy Tales.* London: Octopus Books, 1994.

Andermahr, Sonya. "The Politics of Separatism and Lesbian Utopian Fiction," *New Lesbian Criticism: Literary and Cultural Readings*, ed. Sally Munt. New York: Columbia University Press, 1992.

Arora, Neena. *Nayantara Sahgal and Doris Lessing: A Feminist Study in Comparison.* New Delhi: Prestige Books, 1991.

Barry, Peter. *Beginning Theory: An Introduction to Literary and Cultural Theory.* Manchester and New York: Manchester University Press, 1995.

Basu, Aparna. *Perspectives on Women: Canada and India.* New Delhi: Allied, 1995.

Berry, Kenneth. "The Paradox of Kandinsky's Abstract Representation," *Journal of Aesthetic Education*, 39.1, 2005, 99-104.

Bettelheim, Bruno. *The Uses of Enchantment: The Meaning and Importance of Fairy Tales.* New York: Alfred A. Knopf, 1976.

Boehmer, Elleke. "The Modern Language Review," *The Modern Language Review*, 101.1, 2006, 237-38.

Bose, Amalendu. "Modern Indian Poetry in English," *Indian Literature*, 13.1, 1970, 51-59. www.jstor.org/stable/23329701.

Branicky, Melissa. "Rapunzel, Rapunzel, Let Down Your Hair. . . ," *Room of One's Own: A Space for Women's Writing* , 17.1 (March 1994).

Bunch, Charlotte. "Lesbians as Revolt," *Feminist Theory Reader: Local and Global Perspectives*, ed. Carole R. McCann and Seung Kyung Kim. New York, Routledge, 2003.

Burnside, John. "Marvels & Tales," *Marvels & Tales*, 12.2, 1998, 380-82. www.jstor.org/stable/41388507.

Burt, Sandra, Lorraine Code, and Lindsay Dorney, ed. *Changing Patterns: Women in Canada*. Toronto: The Canadian Publishers, 1993.

Butler, Judith. *Gender Trouble: Feminism and the Subversion of Identity*. New York and London: Routledge, 1990.

Caputi, Jane. "On Psychic Activism: Feminist Mythmaking," *The Feminist Companion to Mythology*, ed. Carolyne Larrington. London: Pandora Press, 1992.

Carter, Albert Howard. "Books Abroad," *Books Abroad*, 42.3, 1968, 488-89. www.jstor.org/stable/40122818.

Chavan, P. Sunanda. *The Fair Voice: A Study of Indian Women Poets in English*. New Delhi: Sterling, 1984.

Clark, J. Elizabeth, and Katie Hogan. "Doing Women's Studies on the Sly at LaGuardia Community College," *Women's Studies Quarterly*, 30.3/4, 2002, 82-89. www.jstor.org/stable/40003245.

Collins, Samuel Gerald. "Sail on! Sail on! Anthropology, Science Fiction, and the Enticing Future," *Science Fiction Studies*, 30.2, Social Science Fiction (July 2003).

Dasgupta, Anannya. "'Do I Remove My Skin?': Interrogating 'Identity' in the Fables of Suniti Namjoshi," *Queering India: Same Sex Love and Eroticism in Indian Culture and Society*, ed. Ruth Vanita. New York: Routledge, 2002.

Das, Prasanta. "Making Things Happen: Poetry, Political and Cultural Change," *Economic and Political Weekly*, 44.36, 2009, 42-44.

Doane, Janice and Devon Hodges. "Tulsa Studies in Women's Literature," *Tulsa Studies in Women's Literature*, 26.2, 2007, 339-42.

Donavan, Josephine. *Feminist Theory: The Intellectual Traditions of American Feminism*. New York: Continuum, 1992.

Dwivedi, A.N. *Papers on Indian Writing in English*. Second Revised and Enlarged Edition. New Delhi: Atlantic, 2001.

Dybikowski, Ann, et al. *In the Feminine: Women and Words = Les Femmes et les mots*. Canada: Longspoon Press, 1985.

Faderman, Lillian. *Surpassing the Love of Men: Romantic Friendship and Love between Women from the Renaissance to the Present*. New York: William Morrow, 1981.

George, Rosemary Marangoly. "'At a Slight Angle to Reality': Reading Indian Diaspora Literature," *MELUS*, 21.3, 1996, 179-93.

Goel, Savita. "Suniti Namjoshi's *Feminist Fables*: A Minor Feminist Classic," *Indian Women Writers: Critical Perspectives*, ed. J.K. Dodiya and K.V. Surendran. New Delhi: Sarup, 1999.

Greene, Elizabeth. "Cinderella's Daughters," *Room of One's Own: A Space for Women's Writing*. 17.1 (March 1994).

Gupta, Tanu. *Indian Women's Poetry: A Study in Schizophrenic Experience*. New Delhi: Prestige Books, 2011,

Gupta, Tanu and Rajni. "Lesbianism as a Revolt: A Study of Suniti Namjoshi," *International Journal of Language, Literature and Humanities*. 3.7, September 2015.

_____. "Diasporic Divulgences and Resultant Resentment: A Study of Suniti Namjoshi," *International Journal of Language, Literature and Humanities*, 20.9, September 2015.

_____. "Women and Patriarchy: A Study of Suniti Namjoshi," *International Journal of Language, Literature and Humanities*, 5.5, October 2015.

Hines, Virginia Lee. "An Old Story," *Room of One's Own: A Space for Women's Writing*. 17.1 (March 1994).

Humm, Maggie, ed. *Feminisms: A Reader*. Great Britain: Harvester Wheatsheaf, 1992.

Irigaray, Luce. "When the Goods Get Together," *Literary Theory*, ed. A.N. Dwivedi. Delhi: Doaba, 2015.

Jagose, Annamarie. *Queer Theory: An Introduction*. New York: New York University Press, 1996.

Johnson, Barbara. *The Feminist Difference: Literature, Psychoanalysis, Race and Gender*. USA: Harvard University Press, 1998.

Kailo, Kaarina. "Refusing to Hold Our Tongues: Women's Folklore, Women's Orality as Self-Recovery," *Room of One's Own: A Space for Women's Writing* 17.1 (March 1994)

Kanaganayakam, Chelva. *Configurations of Exile: South Asian Writers and Their World*. Toronto: TSAR, 1995.

_____. "Exiles and Expatriates," *New National and Post-Colonial Literatures*, ed. Bruce King. Oxford: Clarendon Press, 1996.

Kudchedkar, Shirin. "Feminist Voices from India and Canada," *Feminist Spaces: Cultural Readings from India and Canada*, ed. Malashri Lal. New Delhi: Allied, 1997.

Mark, Marcia. "The Sacrifice and Crackpot: What a Woman can learn by Rewriting a Fairy Tale and Clarifying its Meaning," *Essays on Canadian Writing*, 68 (Summer 1999).

Mahankali, Sandhya. "Themes, Patterns and Attitudes in the Expatriate Indian English Novel: With Particular Reference to the Novel in England, Canada and The United States after 1975," Diss.: Himachal Pradesh U, 1999.

Mandell, Nancy, ed. *Feminist Issues: Race, Class and Sexuality*. Ontario: Prentice Hall Canada, 1995.

Mann, S. Harveen. "Suniti Namjoshi: Diasporic, Lesbian Feminism and the Textual Politics of Transnationality," *The Journal of the Midwest Modern Language Association*, 30.1/2, Borders (Spring 1997).

Mann, Harveen Sachdeva. "U.S. Multiculturalism, Post-Colonialism, and Indo-Anglian Literature: Some Issues of Critical Pedagogy and Theory," *The Journal of the Midwest Modern Language Association*, 27.1, 1994, 94-108. www.jstor.org/stable/1315063.

McGifford, Diane. "Suniti Namjoshi (b. 1941)," *Writers of the Indian Diaspora: A Bio-Bibliographical Critical Source Book*, ed. Emmanuel S. Nelson. USA: Greenwood Press, 1993.

Mishra, Vijay. *The Literature of the Indian Diaspora: Theorizing the Diasporic Imaginary*. New York: Routledge, 2007.

Moi, Toril. *Sexual/Textual Politics: Feminist Literary Theory*. London and New York: Routledge, 1985.

_____. "Feminist, Female, Feminine," *The Feminist Reader: Essays in Gender and the Politics of Literary Criticism*. Hampshire and London: MacMillan, 1989.

Munt, Sally, ed. *New Lesbian Criticism: Literary and Cultural Readings*. New York: Columbia Press, 1992.

Namjoshi, Suniti. *Poems*. Calcutta: Writers Workshop, 1967.

_____. *More Poems*. Calcutta: Writers Workshop, 1971.

_____. *Cyclone in Pakistan*. Calcutta: Writers Workshop, 1971.

_____. *The Jackass and the Lady*. Calcutta: Writers Workshop, 1980.

_____. *The Authentic Lie*. University of New Brunswick: Fiddlehead/Goose Lane Press, 1982.

_____. *From the Bedside Book of Nightmares*. University of New Brunswick: Fiddlehead/Goose Lane Press, 1984.

_____. *The Conversations of Cow*. London Women's Press, 1985.

_____. *Because of India: Selected Poems and Fables*. London: Onlywoman Press, 1989.

_____. *The Blue Donkey Fables*. India: Penguin, 1991.

_____. *The Mothers of Maya Diip*. India: Penguin, 1991.

_____. *Feminist Fables*. India: Penguin, 1995.

_____. *Saint Suniti and the Dragon*. India: Penguin, 1995.

_____. *Building Babel*. North Melbourne: Spinifex, 1996.

_____. *Goja: An Autobiographical Myth*. North Melbourne: Spinifex, 2000.

_____ and Gillian Hanscombe. *Flesh and Paper*. Canada: Ragweed Press, 1988.

Narayan, Shyamala A. "English Scene: Flourishing Signs," *Indian Literature*, 34.1 (141), 1991, 139-46.

_____. "English Scene: Powers of Youth and Manhood Continues," *Indian Literature*, 35.1 (147), 1992, 126-32.

Oakley, Ann. *Sex, Gender and Society*. London: Gower, 1985.

Osborn Jennifer. "Book reviews: The Fabulous Feminist: a Suniti Namjoshi Reader," *Transnational Literature*, 10.2 (May 2018).

Parameswaran, Uma. "Chasm and Bridge: Linguistic and Cultural Barriers between Writer and Community," *Feminist Spaces: Cultural Readings from India and Canada*, ed. Malashri Lal. New Delhi: Allied, 1997.

Paranjape, Makarand. "Distinguishing Themselves: New Fiction by Expatriate Indian Women," *World Literature Today*, 65.1, 1991, 72-74. www.jstor.org/stable/40146126.

_____. "Post-Independence Indian English Literature: Towards a New Literary History," *Economic and Political Weekly*, 33.18, 1998, 1049-56.

Pearson, Wendy. "Science fiction and Queer Theory." http: //www.iml295.com/wp-content/uploads/2017/08/Pearson.pdf

Petievich, Carla. "The Journal of Asian Studies," *The Journal of Asian Studies*, 51.2, 1992, 427-29.

Pfaelzer, Jean and R.M.P. "Parody and Satire in American Dystopian Fiction of the Nineteenth Century (La Parodie et la satire dans la fiction dystopique américaine du XIXème siècle)," *Science Fiction Studies*. 7.1 (March 1980), 61-72.

Putman, Wendy. "Introduction," *Room of One's Own: A Space for Women's Writing*. 17.1 (March 1994).

Ramya D. "Resisting the Fables of Suniti Namjoshi," IRWLE, 11.1, Jan. 2015.

Rankin, Pauline. "A Mermaid Tail," *Room of One's Own: A Space for Women's Writing*. 17.1 (March 1994).

Rath, K. Akshaya. "The Upside-Down Swan: Suniti Namjoshi," *Rupkatha Journal on Interdiscliplinary Studies in Humanities: Special Issue on LGBT and Queer Studies*, VI.1, 2014.

Rich, Adrienne. "Compulsory Heterosexuality and Lesbian Existence," *Signs*, 5 (Summer 1980).

_____. "When We Dead Awaken: Writing as Re-vision," *Adrienne Rich's Poetry and Prose*, ed. Barbara Charlesworth Gelpi and Albert Gelpi. New York: WW Norton, 1993.

Rodríguez, Carolina Fernández. "The Deconstruction of the Male-Rescuer Archetype in Contemporary Feminist Revisions of 'The Sleeping Beauty.'" *Marvels & Tales*, 16.1, 2002, 51-70.

Rooney, Frances. "Tree and Bear," *Room of One's Own: A Space for Women's Writing*, 17.1 (March 1994).

Ross, Oliver. "Other Creatures that have their own identities: Strategic Essentialism in Suniti Namjoshi's Fables," *South Asian Review*, 37.1: 'New Directions in South Asian Canadian Literature and Culture. Guest ed. Chandrima Chakraborty and Robin E. Field.

Ruth, Shiela. *Issues in Feminism: An Introduction to Women's Studies*. California: Mayfield, 1990.

Sanga, Jaina C., ed. *South Asian Novelists in English: An A-Z Guide*. USA: Greenwood Press, 2003.

Sangster, Joan. "Creating Popular Histories: Re-Interpreting 'Second Wave' Canadian Feminism," *Dialectical Anthropology*, 39.4, 2015, 381-404.

Sankey, Gretchen. "Re-viewing the Life and Times of Little Red Riding Hood," *Room of One's Own: A Space for Women's Writing*. 17.1 (March 1994).

Santhanam, Kausalya. "Feminism, one of her voices," *The Hindu*, Sunday, 20 February 2000.

Satchidanandan, K. "Reflections: That Third Space: Interrogating the Diasporic Paradigm," *Indian Literature*, 45.3 (203), 2001, 5-9.

Scheier Libby, Sarah Sheard and Eleanor Wachtel, ed. *Language in her Eye: Views on Writing and Gender by Canadian Women Writing in English*. Toronto: Coach House Press, 1990.

Schwenk, Lorna. "Plucking," *Room of One's Owns: A Space for Women's Writing*. 17.1 (March 1994).

Seager, Joni. "Inhuman Kind," *The Women's Review of Books*, 18.9, 2001, 7-8. www.jstor.org/stable/4023707.

Shahane, Vasant A. "Books Abroad," *Books Abroad*, 47.1, 1973, 219.

Sharma, Kavita A. *The Ongoing Journey: Indian Migration to Canada*. New Delhi: Creative, 1997.

Stacey, Margaret and Marion Price. *Women, Power and Politics*. London and New York: Tavistock, 1981.

Showalter, Elaine, ed. *The New Feminist Criticism: Essays on Women, Literature and Theory*. New York: Pantheon, 1985.

Steinborn, Tamara. "Eve Revisited," *Room of One's Own: A Space for Women's Writing*. 17.1 (March 1994).

Sorrel, Lorraine. "Feminist Fables," *Off Our Backs*, 11.11, 1981, 25. www.jstor.org/stable/25774155.

Somay Bulent and R.M.P., "Towards an Open-Ended Utopia (Vers une utopie ouverte)," *Science Fiction Studies*, 11.1 (March 1984).

Steinisch Sabine. "Subversive Fabulations: The Twofold Pull in Suniti Namjoshi's *Feminist Fables*," *Engendering Realism and Postmodernism: Contemporary Women Writers in Britain*, ed. Beate Neummeier. New York, 2001.

Suvin, Darko. *Positions and Presuppositions in Science Fiction*. Hampshire and London: MacMillan, 1988.

Suzette A. Spencer. "Leaving Home, Coming Home," *The Women's Review of Books*, 19.12, 2002, 20. www.jstor.org/stable/4024066.

Thomas, A.J. "Impressions, Expressions. . . ," *Indian Literature*, 56.1 (267), 2012, 7-14. www.jstor.org/stable/ 23348771.

Vanita, Ruth. "Embracing the Past by Retelling the Stories," *A Sea of Stories: The Shaping Power of Narrative in Gay and Lesbian Cultures*, ed. Sonya L. Jones. New York: Harrington Press, 2000.

Vanita, Ruth. "In the Attic," *Indian Literature*, 56.1 (267), 2012, 220-22.

_____ and Saleem Kidwai, ed. *Same-Sex Love in India: Readings from Literature and History*. New York, Palgrave, 2001.

Vassanji, M.G., ed. *A Meeting of Streams: South Asian Canadian Literature*. Toronto: TSAR, 1985.

Vijayasree. C. *Suniti Namjoshi: The Artful Transgressor*. Jaipur: Rawat, 2001, 72.

Vevaina, Coomi S. "An Interview with Suniti Namjoshi," *ARIEL: A Review of International English Literature*, 29.1 (1998).

Vevaina, Coomi S. and Barbara Godard, ed. *Intersexions: Issues of Race and Gender in Canadian Women's Writing*. New Delhi: Creative, 1996.

Vonarburg, Elizabeth. *The Silent City*, trans. Jane Brierley. Victoria, Canada: Porcépic Books, 1988.

Warfield, Angela. "Revisiting Feminist Utopia," *Science Fiction Studies*, 31.2 (July 2004).

Wegner, Phillip E. "Utopia," *A Companion to Science Fiction*, ed. David Seed. UK: Blackwell, 2008.

Williams, Raymond. "Utopia and Science Fiction," *Science Fiction Studies*, 5.3 (Nov 1978).

York, Lorraine M. "Lesbianizing Authorship: *Flesh and Paper*," *Essays on Canadian Writing: The Gender Issue*, 54 (Winter 1994).

Yorke, Liz. "British Lesbian Poetics: A Brief Exploration," *Feminist Review*, no. 62, 1999, 78-90. www.jstor.org/stable/1395648.

Web Sources

http://gomag.com/article/queer-women-history-forgot-suniti-namjoshi/

https://www.poetryinternationalweb.net/pi/site/poet/item/9964/27/Suniti-Namjoshi

https://www.thehindu.com/2000/02/20/stories/1320129u.htm

https://www.researchgate.net/application.ClientValidation.html?origPath=%2Fpublication%2F282288745_Lesbianism_as_a_Revolt_A_Study_of_Suniti_Namjoshi